Table of Contents

CHAPTER 1 – Course Design

The following general principles of course design list the criteria, responsibilities and restrictions governing course designers as the architects of the sport of USPSA shooting.

1.1 General Principles

1.1.1 **Safety** – USPSA matches must be designed, constructed and conducted with due consideration to safety.

1.1.2 **Quality** – The value of an USPSA match is determined by the quality of the challenge presented in the course design. Courses of fire must be designed primarily to test a competitor's USPSA shooting skills, not their physical abilities.

1.1.3 **Balance** – Accuracy, Power and Speed are equivalent elements of USPSA shooting, and are expressed in the Latin words "Diligentia, Vis, Celeritas" ("DVC"). A properly balanced course of fire will depend largely upon the nature of the challenges presented therein, however, courses must be designed, and USPSA matches must be conducted in such a way, as to evaluate these elements equally.

1.1.4 **Diversity** – USPSA shooting challenges are diverse. While it is not necessary to construct new courses for each match, no single course of fire must be repeated to allow its use to be considered a definitive measure of USPSA shooting skills.

1.1.5 **Freestyle** – USPSA matches are freestyle. Competitors must be permitted to solve the challenge presented in a freestyle manner, and to shoot targets on an "as and when visible" basis. (In a Multigun course of fire the course description must define which targets are to be shot with which type of firearm and may specify the order in which the different firearms must be used.) Courses of fire must not require mandatory reloads nor dictate a shooting position, stance or location, except as stated below. However, conditions may be created, and barriers or other physical limitations may be constructed, to compel a competitor into shooting positions, locations or stances.

1.1.5.1 Because of the physical difficulty making courses that involve long range rifle targets totally freestyle course designs may restrict where to engage and reengage long range targets. This must be done by a) requiring contact with a prop, b) requiring shooting through a specific port or c) requiring shooting from a designated area or location. Course designs may not dictate how these locations must be used. A long-range target is defined as a target 50 yards and further.

1.1.5.2 Multigun course designers may present challenges which provide the shooter options with regard to firearm use within the context of a multigun stage. Any such options must comply with Rule 2.1.3 and Section 3.2.

    1.1.5.3   Level I matches may use shooting boxes and specify where or when specific target arrays may be engaged.

    1.1.5.4   Speed shoots and Standard Exercises may include mandatory reloads and may dictate a shooting position, location or stance.

    1.1.5.5   Speed shoots and Standard Exercises may specify shooting the handgun using the strong hand or weak hand unsupported. The specified hand must be used exclusively from the point stipulated for the remainder of the string or stage. Shotgun, Rifle, and Pistol Caliber Carbine Speed shoots and Standard Exercises may specify the use of the strong or weak shoulder.

1.1.6   **Difficulty** – USPSA matches present varied degrees of difficulty. No shooting challenge or time limit may be appealed as being prohibitive. This does not apply to non-shooting challenges, which should reasonably allow for differences in a competitor's height and physical build.

1.1.7   **Scenarios and Stage Props** – The use of scenarios and reasonable stage props is encouraged. Care must be exercised, however, to avoid unrealistic non-shooting requirements which detract from the shooting challenge and/or may expose competitors to potentially unsafe conditions.

1.2   Types of Courses

USPSA matches for Rifle, Shotgun, or Multigun may contain the following types of courses of fire. (Note: These rules may not be used to run a handgun only or PCC only match. Such matches are governed by a different rule book.):

1.2.1   **General Courses of Fire** – Match officials are free to design any course of fire that complies with the requirements of Chapters 2 through 4 and scored by an acceptable method per Chapter 9. Note that the scoring method selected from Chapter 9 must be the same for all stages in the match. (i.e., You may not use Comstock for some courses and Time Plus for others.)

    1.2.1.1   Rifle or Shotgun matches must only use courses designed for that specific firearm type, i.e., Rifle or Shotgun.

    1.2.1.2   Multigun matches must use at least two different firearm types within the match and, preferably, should include two or more firearm types in each course of fire. A multigun match may occasionally use a stage designed for only one specific firearm type but must not do this for the majority of the match.

1.2.2   **Special Courses of Fire**

    1.2.2.1   **Standard Exercises** – Courses of fire consisting of two or more separately timed component strings. Scores, with any penalties deducted, are accumulated on completion of the course of fire to produce the final stage results. The course of fire for each component string may require a specific shooting position, procedure and/or one or more mandatory reloads.

1.2.2.1.1 For Rifle or Shotgun matches – Standard Exercises must not require more than 32 rounds to complete. Component strings must not require more than 8 rounds (16 rounds if a mandatory reload is specified). Separate target arrays for each string are strongly encouraged.

1.2.2.1.2 For Multigun matches – Standard Exercises must not require more than 48 rounds to complete and should incorporate two or more firearm types. Component strings must not require more than 8 rounds per firearm (16 rounds if a mandatory reload is specified for that firearm). Component strings may require individual firearm types or multiple firearm types.

1.2.2.2 **Speed Shoot** – Courses of fire consisting of one continuous string of fire shot on one or more arrays of multiple targets from a single location or view. The written stage briefing may specify engaging arrays of targets without violating rule 1.1.5), as long as the competitor is allowed to engage said arrays in any order, and individual target engagement is not specified.

1.2.2.2.1 For Rifle or Shotgun matches – No more than eight rounds may be required without a mandatory reload and no more than one mandatory reload may be required in the course of fire. No more than 16 rounds total may be required. Weak/Strong shoulder may be stipulated after the reload is complete.

1.2.2.2.2 For Multigun matches – No more than eight rounds per firearm type may be required. (The transition from one firearm type to another will be used instead of mandatory reloads.) Total rounds are limited by the number of firearm types required in the Course of Fire times 8. Weak/Strong hand/shoulder may not be stipulated for a speed shoot in a multigun match prior to the final firearm used for the Course of Fire.

1.3   USPSA Sanctioning

1.3.1   Match organizers wishing to receive Level II or Level III USPSA sanction must comply with the general principles of course design and course construction as well as all other current USPSA rules and regulations relevant to the discipline. Courses of fire that do not comply with these requirements will not be sanctioned and must not be publicized or announced as USPSA sanctioned matches. Match organizers applying for USPSA Level II or III sanction agree to post their results to the USPSA web page as soon as possible upon completion of the match, regardless of the scoring system used.

1.3.2   The Director of NROI, his delegate, or an officer of the Organization (in that order) may withdraw USPSA sanctioning from a match. Such action may be taken at any time where, in his or their opinion, a match contravenes the purpose or spirit of the principles of course design or is in breach of any of the current USPSA Rules or is likely to bring the sport of USPSA shooting into disrepute.

1.3.3   USPSA match level requirements and recommendations are specified in Appendix A1.

CHAPTER 2 – Course Construction, Equipment and Modification

The following general regulations of course construction list the criteria, responsibilities and restrictions applicable to courses of fire in USPSA matches. Course designers, host organizations and officials are governed by these regulations.

2.1 General Regulations

2.1.1 **Physical Construction** – Safety considerations in the design, physical construction, and stated requirements for any course of fire are the responsibility of the host organization subject to the approval of the Range Master. Reasonable effort must be made to prevent injury to competitors, officials and spectators during the match. Course design should prevent inadvertent unsafe actions wherever possible. Consideration must be given to the operation of any course of fire to provide suitable access for officials supervising the competitors.

2.1.2 **Safe Angles of Fire** – Courses of fire must always be constructed to ensure safe angles of fire. Consideration must be given to safe target and frame construction and the angle of any possible ricochets. Where appropriate the physical dimensions and suitability of backstops and side berms must be determined as part of the construction process.

2.1.3 **Minimum Distances** – Minimum distances for any metal target or metal hard cover are specific for that firearm type, in feet:

	Barrier	Fault Line
Handgun or PCC	23	26
Shotgun Plates (bird & buckshot)	16	19
Shotgun Poppers (bird & buckshot)	16	19
Shotgun (slugs)	147	150
Rifle	147	150

Where possible, this should be done with physical barriers. If Fault Lines are used to limit the approach to metal targets, they must be placed in such a way that the competitor may inadvertently fault the line and still be outside the minimum distance. (See Rule 10.5.16) Care should also be taken in respect of metal props in the line of fire.

2.1.4 Stage designs must be configured in so that firearms, when staged or abandoned, are pointed downrange, and positioned in such a way that no person is ever allowed or required to pass in front of the muzzle of a staged firearm.

2.1.5 **Target Locations** – When a course is constructed to include target locations other than immediately downrange, organizers and officials must protect or restrict surrounding areas to which competitors, officials or spectators have access. Each competitor must be allowed to solve the competitive problem in his own way and must not be hindered by being forced to act in any manner which might cause unsafe action. Targets must be arranged so that shooting at them on an "as and when visible" basis will not cause competitors to breach safe angles of fire.

2.1.6 **Range Surface** – Where possible, the range surface must be prepared prior to the match, and be kept moderately clear of debris during the match to provide reasonable safety for competitors and officials. Consideration should be given to the possibility of inclement weather and competitor actions. Range Officials may add gravel, sand or other materials to a deteriorated range surface at any time and such range maintenance actions cannot be appealed by competitors.

2.1.7 **Obstacles** – Natural or created obstacles in a course of fire should reasonably allow for variations in competitors' heights and physical builds and should be constructed to provide reasonable safety for all competitors, Match Officials and spectators.

2.1.8 **Target Placement** – Care must be taken with the physical placement of a cardboard target to prevent a "shoot through."

2.1.8.1 When cardboard and metal targets are used in close proximity in a course of fire, care must be taken to minimize the risk of splatter from metal targets.

2.1.8.2 When Poppers are used in a course of fire, care should be taken to ensure that the location or foundation area is prepared to provide consistent operation throughout the match.

2.1.8.3 Static IPSC cardboard targets must not be presented at an angle greater than approximately 45 degrees from the vertical. No-shoot static IPSC cardboard targets may be presented at any angle.

2.1.8.4 Appearing scoring targets should be designed and constructed to be obscured to the competitor (during the course of fire) prior to activation. If the entire target is not obscured, it may be shot at any time during the course of fire, whether activated or not.

2.1.8.4.1 Level I matches are encouraged but not required to comply with this requirement. The Written Stage Briefing must specify any targets that must be activated before being engaged.

2.1.9 All berms are "off limits" to all persons at all times, except when access to them is specifically permitted by a Range Officer. (See Rule 10.3.1.)

2.2 Course Construction Criteria

During the construction of a course of fire, a variety of physical barriers may be used to restrict competitor movement and to provide additional competitive challenges as follows:

2.2.1   Competitor movement may be restricted or controlled through the use of physical barriers, Fault Lines, Shooting Boxes, or Off-Limits Lines.

    2.2.1.1   Shooting Boxes and Fault Lines should be constructed of wooden boards or other suitable material, must be fixed firmly in place, and provide both physical and visual references to competitors. For hard ground surfaces clear of debris, 0.75-inch material is the minimum allowable size. On other range surfaces, such as covered with turf, sand, gravel, wood chips or similar, thicker material which rises at least 1.5 inches above the surface is recommended.

    2.2.1.2   A 'shooting area' is defined as a surface inside shooting boxes, fault lines, walls, or any other barrier. Shooting boxes and fault lines must be fixed to the surface and may not be less than the minimum height required by rule 2.2.1.1. Fault lines are considered to be part of the shooting area. Objects completely outside the shooting area, regardless of whether they contact the shooting box, fault lines, walls, or any other barrier, are not part of the shooting area, except as specified in 10.2.1. Course designers may specify planks, timbers, low platforms, etc., as the entire shooting area, provided they are clearly marked, are at least 1.5" high, and stable.

    2.2.1.3   Fault Lines extending rearward (uprange) should be a minimum of 3 feet in length, and unless otherwise stated in the written stage briefing, are deemed to extend rearward to infinity.

    2.2.1.4   The use of rear fault lines at prone shooting positions should be avoided or used with caution. If a rear fault line is used, it must be placed at least 8 feet from the forward fault line at the prone shooting position.

    2.2.1.5   **Off-Limits Lines** may be used to define an area of the range floor which has been declared off-limits. The written stage briefing must identify the presence and location of Off-Limits Lines, if any. The off-limits area must be clearly delineated with rope, caution tape or other materials and must be at least 2 feet high and at least 2 feet from any Fault Line or Shooting Box. Crossing an off-limits line will result in a zero for the stage. Openings in off-limits lines are allowed for RO access only; competitors may not use the openings to enter any off-limits areas or move through the course of fire in a manner not indicated by the off-limits lines. The lines are deemed to extend through the open areas.

2.2.2   **Obstacles** – Courses of fire may include the use of barriers or major obstacles to be surmounted by competitors. Obstacles used in this way must not exceed a height of 6.5 feet. Obstacles over 3 feet in height must be supplied with scaling aids to assist competitors and must be constructed to provide for the competitor's safety in the following ways:

2.2.2.1 Obstacles must be firmly anchored and braced to provide adequate support when in use. Wherever possible, unduly sharp or rough surfaces must be removed to reduce the possibility of injury to competitors and/or Match Officials.

2.2.2.2 The descending side of any obstacle must be clear of obstructions or natural hazards.

2.2.2.3 Competitors must be allowed to test such obstacles before the course of fire and should be given a short period to do so.

2.2.2.4 Competitors must not be required to holster their handgun before ascending these obstacles.

2.2.3 **Barriers** – Must be constructed in the following manner:

2.2.3.1 They must be high enough and strong enough to serve the intended purpose.

2.2.3.2 They should include Fault Lines projecting rearward at ground level from the side edges.

2.2.3.3 Unless otherwise specified in the Written Stage Briefing any barriers, walls, vision barriers, barrels, snow-fence barriers and other constructs which are 5'9" tall or taller will be considered to go from ground to infinity. Unless otherwise specified in the stage briefing, any walls, vision barriers, barrels, snow-fence barriers and other constructs less than 5'9" tall will be considered to go from ground to height built. Any barrier under 5'9" tall that is to be considered as extending to infinity must be marked accordingly.

2.2.3.4 All such barriers are considered to represent a solid plane and are considered hard cover unless designated as soft cover (see 9.1.6). Shots cannot be fired though the barrier except at designated shooting ports or other designated openings. Any hits that result from full diameter shots fired through a barrier except through a designated port or opening will not count for score and if a steel target is knocked down it will be considered REF and a reshoot will be ordered. See 9.1.6.2

2.2.3.5 All supports for barriers or raised platforms are considered to be non-existent and cannot be used for support. This rule does not apply to obstacles under 2.2.2.

2.2.4   **Tunnels** – A tunnel that a competitor is required to enter or pass through must be constructed of suitable material and to any length. However, sufficient ports must be provided to allow Match Officials to safely monitor competitor action. Tunnel mouth edges must be prepared to minimize the possibility of injury to competitors and Match Officials. Course designers must clearly designate the entrance and exit portions of the tunnel as well as the parameters for shooting at any targets from within the tunnel (e.g., Fault Lines).

2.2.5   **"Cooper" Tunnels** – These are tunnels comprised of braced uprights supporting loose overhead materials (e.g., wooden slats) which may be inadvertently dislodged by competitors. (See Rule 10.2.5.) These tunnels may be constructed to any height, but overhead materials must not be heavy enough to cause injury if they fall.

2.2.6   **Stage Props** – Where these items are intended to support a competitor in motion or while shooting targets, they must be constructed with the safety of the competitor and Match Officials as a priority. Provisions must be made to allow Match Officials to safely monitor and control competitor action at all times. Props must be strong enough to withstand use by all competitors.

2.2.7   Stages that require abandoning a firearm must provide a device which retains the firearm in a safe and stable position and orientation. Examples of suitable devices include boxes (with or without lids) which have sides high enough to prevent the firearm from being dislodged; tubes or barrels arranged to hold the firearm in place, etc. Any such devices must be securely fixed in a safe position and orientation, so that a firearm placed within is pointed towards a berm or other safe direction, cannot easily or inadvertently be dislodged, and so that no person may pass in front of the muzzle of a firearm placed in the device.

2.2.8   Competitors may be required to use a prop gun supplied by the Match Director on a stage to start the course of fire. It may not be required to engage more than three (3) targets before abandoning it. The prop gun and all related ammunition and equipment will be provided by the host match officials and be the same for all competitors.

2.3   Modifications to Course Construction

2.3.1   Match Officials may, for any reason, modify the physical construction or stage procedure for a course of fire, provided that such changes are approved in advance by the Range Master. Any such physical changes or additions to a published course of fire should be completed before the stage begins.

2.3.1.1   In lieu of modifying course design or physical construction, a Range Master may explicitly forbid certain competitor actions in order to maintain safety during a course of fire.

Declaration of a Forbidden Action may be made to prohibit competitor movement which is likely to result in an unsafe condition.

The declaration of a Forbidden Action cannot be used as a means of compelling or limiting competitor movement within a course of fire (e.g., to prevent a shooter from "cutting the corner" on an L-shaped shooting area). Except as provided in Rule 1.1.5.1, a course designer wishing to compel, or limit competitor movement must do so using target placement, vision barriers, physical barriers, or off-limits lines.

Subject to the above, an area of the range floor may be declared off-limits. The area must be clearly delineated with Off-Limits Lines (Rule 2.2.1.5). Crossing an Off-Limits Line will result in a zero for the stage.

Any Forbidden Action or Off-Limits Area must be specified in the Written Stage Briefing (See Rules 2.3.3 and 3.2.3).

2.3.2 All competitors must be notified of any such changes as soon as possible. As a minimum, they must be notified by the official in charge of the course of fire during the squad briefing.

2.3.3 If the Range Master approves any such action after the match begins, he must either:

2.3.3.1 Allow the course of fire to continue with the modification affecting only those competitors who have not already completed the stage. If a competitor's actions caused the change, that competitor must be required to reshoot the altered course of fire; or

2.3.3.2 If possible, require all competitors to complete the course of fire as revised with all previous attempts removed from the match scores.

2.3.3.3 A competitor who refuses to reshoot a course of fire, under this or any other section, when so ordered by a Range Official, will receive a zero score for that stage, irrespective of any previous attempt.

2.3.4 If the Range Master (in consultation with the Match Director) determines that the physical or procedural change results in a loss of competitive equity and it is impossible for all competitors to attempt the revised stage, or if the stage has been rendered unsuitable or unworkable for any reason, that stage and all associated competitor scores must be deleted from the match.

2.3.5 During inclement weather, the Range Master may order that cardboard targets be fitted with transparent protective covers, treated/waterproof targets, and/or overhead shelters, and this order is not subject to appeal by competitors. (See Rule 6.5.1.) Such items must be applied and remain fitted to all affected targets for the same period of time, until the order is rescinded by the Range Master.

2.3.6   If the Range Master (in consultation with the Match Director) deems that climatic or other conditions have, or are likely to, seriously affect the safety and/or conduct of a match, he may order that all shooting activities be suspended, until he issues a "resume shooting" directive.

2.4   Long Gun Bagging/Unbagging/Staging Area

2.4.1   A bagging/un-bagging/staging area must be provided for every stage or shooting bay, to facilitate bagging, un-bagging, and staging of long guns. This area may take the form of a rack or table or both. All firearms in the staging area must have their actions locked open or have chamber flags inserted with the bolt closed on them or be cased/bagged. This area may be used for holstered or cased/bagged handguns, see 5.2.1.1. Handguns may only be handled in a Safety Area (see 2.6).

2.4.2   Such areas must be marked with adequate signage to indicate their purpose. Fault lines or flagging should be employed. These areas MUST be adjacent to a berm so that shooters may bag/un-bag without sweeping people and must be as close to the berm as possible, to prevent persons from traveling between the staged long guns and the berm.

2.4.3   Bagging/Unbagging/Staging Areas must never be immediately adjacent to a Safety Area.

2.5   Shotgun Preload Area

2.5.1   Any stage requiring the use of a shotgun may have a shotgun preloading table set up. (*See 8.3.1.3 for guidance.*) Rifles or Pistol Caliber Carbines and cased/holstered/bagged handguns may also be staged on, by, or under the preload table if space permits. See 2.4.1 and 5.2.1.1.

2.5.2   Long Gun Staging Areas and/or Shotgun Preload Tables must never be immediately adjacent to a Safety Area.

2.6   Safety Areas

2.6.1   The host organization is responsible for the construction and placement of a sufficient number of Safety Areas for the match. They should be conveniently placed and easily identified with signs. Safety Areas must include a table with the safe direction and boundaries clearly shown. Safety Areas must never be immediately adjacent to any Long Gun Bagging/Unbagging Area, Staging Area, or Shotgun Preload Table.

2.6.2   Competitors are permitted to use the Safety Areas for the activities stated below provided they remain completely within the boundaries of the Safety

Area and the firearm is pointed in a safe direction. Violations are subject to match disqualification.

2.6.2.1   Casing, uncasing, and holstering unloaded firearms.

2.6.2.2   Practice the mounting, drawing, "dry-firing" and re-holstering of unloaded firearms.

2.6.2.3   Practice the insertion and removal of empty magazines and/or to cycle the action of a firearm.

2.6.2.4   Conduct inspections, stripping, cleaning, repairs and maintenance of firearms, component parts and other accessories.

2.6.3   Dummy ammunition (including practice or training rounds, snap caps and empty cases), loaded magazines, loaded speed loading devices and live rounds must not be handled in a Safety Area under any circumstances.

2.7   Unloading/Loading Station

2.7.1   If it is possible that some competitors arriving at a range where a USPSA match is being held may be in possession of a loaded firearm on their person (e.g. law enforcement officers, persons duly authorized to carry a loaded firearm, etc.), match organizers should provide an Unloading/Loading Station to enable such competitors to safely unload their firearms prior to entering the range, and to safely load their firearms again on departure from the range. The Unloading/Loading Station should be conveniently located outside the entrance to the range (or outside the portion of the range allocated to the USPSA match), it should be clearly marked with a sign and it must include a suitable impact zone.

2.7.2   Where no Unloading/Loading station is provided, a competitor who arrives at a match in possession of a loaded firearm and proceeds immediately to a match official for the express purpose of safely unloading the firearm shall not be subject to disqualification per the provisions of Rule 10.5.12.

CHAPTER 3 – Course Information

3.1   General Regulations

The competitor is always responsible to safely fulfill the requirements of a course of fire but can only reasonably be expected to do so after verbally or physically receiving the written stage briefing, which must adequately explain the requirements to the competitors.

3.1.1   Published Courses of Fire – Registered competitors must be provided with the same course of fire information, within the same notice period, in advance of the match. The information may be provided by physical or electronic means, or by reference to a website (also see Section 2.3).

3.1.2   Non-Published Course of Fire – Same as Rule 3.1.1 except that the details for the course of fire are not published beforehand. The stage instructions are provided in the written stage briefing.

3.2   Written Stage Briefings

3.2.1   A written stage briefing approved by the Range Master must be posted at each course of fire prior to commencement of the match. This briefing will take precedence over any course of fire information published or otherwise communicated to competitors in advance of the match, and it must provide the following minimum information:

— Scoring Method
— Any time limits for Limited Time Comstock stages or Time Plus stages:
— Targets (type & number)
— Minimum number of rounds
— Ammunition type or types that are acceptable or required (shotgun)
— Start position (This should be demonstrated by a Range Officer)
— When time starts/stops: audible or visual signal
— Procedure
— Identification of specific targets to be shot with specific firearms (e.g., T1-T4 are to be engaged with Handgun, T5-T8 with Rifle, T9-10 with either).
— Location and ready condition for all firearms used on the stage
— Designation of locations and conditions where firearms may be abandoned
— Need for a Shooter Delegate to observe the RO clearing firearms during the course of fire (See Rule 8.4.2.3).

3.2.2   The Range Official in charge of a course of fire must read out the written stage briefing verbatim to each squad.

3.2.3   The Range Master may modify a written stage briefing at any time for reasons of clarity, consistency or safety. (See Section 2.3.)

3.2.4   After the written stage briefing has been read to competitors and questions arising there from have been answered, competitors should be permitted to conduct an orderly inspection ("walkthrough") of the course of fire. The duration of time for the inspection must be stipulated by the Range Officer and it should be the same for all competitors. If the course of fire includes moving targets or similar items, these should be demonstrated to all competitors for the same duration and frequency.

3.2.5   A written stage briefing must comply with the current USPSA rules.

3.2.6   In the event that a competitor action contravenes the course requirements, and that action creates a safety issue, the Range Master must be immediately summoned for a ruling. The Range Master may rule that the action is allowed, and the competitor's score will stand. Alternatively, the Range Master may require modifications to the course of fire, and/or may declare that the action is "forbidden" for safety reasons. (See Rule 2.3, including subsections)

    3.2.6.1   Following the declaration of a Forbidden Action, the shooter(s) whose action(s) resulted in such a declaration shall be required to reshoot the course of fire. Subsequent violations by any competitor will result in a disqualification. See 10.3.6.

3.3   Applicability of the Rules

USPSA matches are governed by the rules applicable to the discipline. Host organizations may not enforce local rules except to comply with legislation or legal precedent in the applicable jurisdiction. Any voluntarily adopted rules that are not in compliance with these rules must not be applied to USPSA matches without the express written consent of the President of USPSA. All local rules allowed under these provisions will be documented at USPSA HQ.

3.3.1   In states where competitors are restricted by law to maximum magazine capacity, that maximum capacity will be the maximum allowed for all competitors in the contest. Any such limitations must be made known to all competitors by the Match Director/Range Master before the start of the match.

CHAPTER 4 – Range Equipment

4.1   Targets – General Principles

4.1.1   Only targets listed in Appendices B may be used for USPSA Rifle, Shotgun, or Multigun matches. Only official, USPSA-licensed cardboard targets may be used.

4.1.2   Scoring targets used in all USPSA Rifle, Shotgun, or Multigun matches must be of a single color, as follows:

    4.1.2.1   The scoring area of scoring cardboard targets must be of a brown or tan cardboard color.

    4.1.2.2   The entire front of scoring metal targets must be painted a single color, preferably white. Shotgun targets may be unpainted.

    4.1.2.3   Self-indicating metal scoring targets need not be painted after each competitor.

4.1.3   No-shoots must be clearly marked or be of a single color different from scoring targets. Metal no-shoots in the general size and shape of authorized cardboard targets may be used. Metal no-shoots do not have a non-scoring border.

4.1.4   Targets used in a course of fire may be partially or wholly hidden through the use of hard or soft cover:

    4.1.4.1   Cover provided to hide all or a portion of a target will be considered hard cover. When possible, hard cover should not be simulated but constructed using impenetrable materials (see Rule 2.1.3). Whole cardboard targets must not be used solely as hard cover.

    4.1.4.2   Cover provided merely to obscure targets is considered soft cover. Shots which have passed through soft cover and which strike a scoring target will score. Shots that have passed through soft cover before hitting a no-shoot will be penalized. All scoring zones on targets hidden by soft cover must be left wholly intact. Targets obscured by soft cover must either be visible through the soft cover or a portion of the affected target(s) must be visible from around or over the soft cover. Use of soft cover to obscure Shotgun targets is prohibited.

    4.1.4.3   No target or no-shoot target, be it cardboard, metal, or frangible, may be designed, manufactured, or modified such that it has a hole in its scoring surface through which rounds may pass without striking the surface of the target.

4.1.5   Declaring a single, intact target to represent two or more targets by use of tape, paint or any other means is prohibited.

4.2 Approved Targets – Cardboard

4.2.1 There are two types of cardboard targets approved for use in all levels of USPSA matches, the IPSC target and the USPSA target. (See Appendix B1.) Half-sized versions of either target are allowed for all level matches in Rifle, Shotgun, and Multigun, subject to the following:

4.2.1.1 Half-sized USPSA targets can be covered with hard cover or no-shoots as long as 50% or more of the **lower** A-zone is visible.

4.2.1.2 Half-sized IPSC targets can be covered with hard cover or no-shoots as long as 50% or more of the A-zone is visible (see Appendix B1).

4.2.1.3 Half-sized targets may not be mounted onto full-sized no-shoot targets or used as no-shoots on full-sized scoring targets.

4.2.1.4 Restrictions on angle of placement still apply for IPSC targets. See the dimensions in the drawings.

4.2.2 Cardboard targets must have scoring lines and non-scoring borders clearly marked on the face of the target.

4.2.2.1 The face of cardboard no-shoots must include a sufficiently distinguishable non-scoring border. In the absence of perforations or other suitable markings, the Range Master must order that all affected targets have a replacement non-scoring border drawn or fitted thereon.

4.2.3 Cardboard targets must never be required to receive more than 12 hits before being scored and patched.

4.2.4 When the scoring area of a cardboard target is to be partially hidden, course designers must simulate hard cover in one of the following ways:

4.2.4.1 By actually hiding a portion of the target (see Rule 4.1.4.1).

4.2.4.2 By physically cutting targets to remove the portion deemed to be hidden by hard cover. Such targets must be fitted with a replacement non-scoring border, which must extend the full width of the cut scoring area (see Rule 4.2.2).

4.2.4.3 By painting or taping the portion of the target deemed to be hidden by hard cover a single and visibly contrasting color.

4.2.5 Hard Cover (and overlapping no-shoots) must not completely hide the highest scoring zone on a partially hidden cardboard target. The minimum requirements are specified in Appendix B1.

4.3 Approved Targets – Metal

4.3.1 Approved metal targets for use in USPSA Multigun matches include any metal target that provides an adequate method of determining hits which includes falling or self-indicating (flashers). Scoring metal targets by listening for hits is not permitted. Fixed metal targets where hits can be visually verified, like slug or close rifle targets, are approved inside of 100 yards. RO may call hits.

4.3.2 Self-resetting targets, when used in a COF, may be engaged from multiple shooting locations as new targets.

4.3.3 All types of approved metal targets may be used as scoring targets or no-shoots.

4.3.4 Poppers and Mini Poppers are approved targets designed to recognize power and must be calibrated as specified in Appendix C1. Visible evidence of a hit must be present to calibrate the popper. If no evidence is present, the request for calibration shall be denied.

4.3.5 Unlike Poppers, metal plates are not subject to calibration or calibration challenges. If a scoring metal plate for PCC, handgun or rifle has been hit but fails to fall or overturn, the Range Officer shall declare range equipment failure and order the competitor to reshoot the course of fire, after the faulty plate has been rectified. Metal scoring shotgun plates will be scored as a hit if the plate falls or overturns from a hit on the plate, base, or supporting stand when the plate is shot at. Hits with a shotgun which do not cause the plate to fall or overturn are not considered range equipment failure. Shotgun plates must fall to score.

> **4.3.5.1** For PCC, rifle and pistol plates only: A plate that has been hit a second time and falls or overturns before a Range Officer can stop the competitor will be scored as hit and there will be no reshoot issued.

4.3.6 Metal no-shoot targets must, if hit, be repainted after each competitor ends their attempt at the course of fire, failing which subsequent competitors must not be penalized for hits visible on their surface.

4.4 Frangible and Synthetic Targets

4.4.1 Frangible and Synthetic Targets are approved for USPSA Rifle, Shotgun, and Multigun (PCC, Rifle and Shotgun targets only) matches. (See Rule 9.5.4.)

4.5 Rearrangement of Range Equipment or Surface

4.5.1 The competitor must not interfere with the range surface, natural foliage, constructions, props or other range equipment (including targets, target stands and target activators) at any time. Violations may incur one procedural penalty per occurrence at the discretion of the Range Officer.

4.5.1.1   Exception - a competitor is allowed to move stone, sand or other loose material at the starting position for the purposes of achieving level and stable footing.

4.5.2   The competitor may request that Match Officials take corrective actions to ensure consistency in respect of the range surface, the presentation of targets and/or any other matter. The Range Master will have final authority concerning all such requests.

4.6   Range Equipment Failure and Other Issues

4.6.1   Range equipment must present the challenge fairly and equitably to all competitors. Range equipment failure includes but is not limited to: the displacement of cardboard targets, the premature activation of metal or moving targets, the failure to reset moving targets or steel targets, the malfunction of mechanically or electrically operated equipment, and the failure of props such as openings, ports, and barriers.

4.6.2   A competitor who is unable to complete a course of fire due to range equipment failure, or if a metal or moving target was not reset prior to his attempt at a course of fire, must be required to reshoot the course of fire after corrective actions have been taken.

4.6.3   Chronic malfunction of equipment in a course of fire may result in the removal of that stage from the match results (see Rule 2.3.4).

4.6.4   If a prop gun provided malfunctions or fails, the competitor will be stopped immediately and given a reshoot once the malfunction has been repaired.

CHAPTER 5 – Competitor Equipment

5.1 Firearms

5.1.1 Firearms are separated and defined by Divisions. (See <u>Appendices D1 to D5</u>.) However, courses of fire must remain consistent for all Divisions.

5.1.2 A firearm is considered to be the combination of a specific caliber/gauge, barrel, stock or grip, sighting system, and fixed magazine or magazine tube if applicable. Competitors must not reconfigure any firearm (i.e., change caliber/gauge, barrel, muzzle brakes/compensator/flash hiders, butt stock, forend, sighting system {including scopes, magnifiers, etc.} fixed magazine or magazine tube) during the course of a match. (See Rule <u>5.1.9</u>.)

    5.1.2.1 Handguns with shoulder stocks and/or fore grips of any kind are prohibited. Rifles, PCCs and Shotguns must be fitted with a stock, enabling them to be fired from the shoulder.

    5.1.2.2 Chokes, slings, bi-pods, monopods, ammo/mag holders, and flashlights may be added, removed or changed at any time during the match, providing that they are allowed in the competitor's division.

    5.1.2.3 Choke tubes and other choke-altering devices are permitted.

5.1.3 The minimum cartridge case dimension for handguns or PCCs to be used in USPSA matches is 9x19 mm. The minimum bullet diameter is 9 mm (.354 inches.) The minimum caliber for Rifle is 5.45mm x 39mm. Shotguns must be 20 gauge or larger. Some divisions may have a higher minimum.

5.1.4 **Sights** – Types of sights identified by USPSA are:

    5.1.4.1 "Open sights" - aiming devices fitted to a firearm which do not use electronic circuitry and/or lenses.

    5.1.4.2 "Optical/electronic sights" - aiming devices fitted to a firearm that use electronic circuitry and/or lenses.

        5.1.4.2.1 A magnifier may be used with an optical sight in Tactical Divisions without violating the "one optic" rule, provided:

            — The magnifier does not contain an aiming reticle.
            — The magnifier cannot be used as an aiming device by itself.
            — The magnifier is mounted in the same location on the rifle for the entire match. If these provisions are satisfied the magnifier will not be considered a second/separate optic and the competitor may start and use their optic in either magnified or

unmagnified mode without restriction.

5.1.4.3 The Range Master is the final authority in respect of the classification of any sights used in an USPSA match and/or their compliance with these rules, including the Divisions in <u>Appendices D1 to D5</u>.

5.1.5 There is no restriction on the trigger pull weight; however, the trigger mechanism must at all times function safely.

5.1.6 Triggers and/or trigger shoes that extend beyond the width of the trigger guard are expressly prohibited on a handgun. However, rifles and shotguns fitted with "winter triggers/guards" may be used in this mode, provided that this fitting was designed, manufactured and provided as part of the firearm and only when the particular climate or weather conditions dictate their use.

5.1.7 All firearms must be serviceable and safe. Range Officers may demand examination of a competitor's firearm or related equipment at any time to check they are functioning safely. If any such item is declared unserviceable or unsafe by a Range Officer, it must be withdrawn from the match until the item is repaired to the satisfaction of the Range Master.

5.1.8 Competitors must use the same firearm and sighting system for all courses of fire in a match (the same handgun, rifle, shotgun, PCC, etc.) However, in the event that a competitor's original firearm and/or sighting system become unserviceable or unsafe during a match, the competitor must, before using a substitute firearm and/or sighting system, seek permission from the Range Master who may approve the substitution provided he is satisfied:

5.1.8.1 The substitute satisfies the requirements of the relevant Division and, in the case of a rifle, is of the same type, action, and caliber, fitted with the same type of sights.

5.1.8.2 In using the substitute, the competitor will not gain a competitive advantage.

5.1.8.3 The competitor's replacement firearm and its appropriate ammunition must be chronographed, regardless of whether or not the original was previously tested. (Does not apply to shotguns or time plus scoring.)

5.1.8.4 If the original firearm/ammunition was not previously tested, and if the original firearm has already been used on a stage and can be safely fired (i.e. the malfunction is not related to an inability to safely fire the firearm), then the original firearm and its ammunition supply remain subject to testing. (Does not apply to shotguns or time plus scoring.)

5.1.9 A competitor who substitutes or significantly modifies a firearm during a match without the prior approval of the Range Master will be subject to disqualification for unsportsmanlike conduct. (See Rule 10.6.1.)

5.1.10   Competitors may be required to carry more than one firearm at a time but must never be required or allowed to engage targets with more than one firearm at a time. (See Rule 8.4.2.2.)

5.1.11   Handguns offering "burst" and/or fully automatic operation are prohibited. Rifles and PCCs offering only "burst" and/or fully automatic operation (i.e., whereby more than one round can be discharged on a single pull or activation of the trigger) are prohibited. Use of trigger systems that allow one round to be fired upon pulling the trigger and another on releasing the trigger is prohibited. Full auto, burst fire, mechanically aided bump fire, and binary fire will result in a procedural on the first instance, and a disqualification for any subsequent occurrences. (Unsafe Gun Handling, see 10.5.18.)

5.1.12   Sound suppressors are not allowed on any firearm, nor may they be used as or in lieu of a compensator.

5.2   Carry and Storage of Competitor Equipment

5.2.1   Handguns

5.2.1.1   Except when within the boundaries of a safety area or when under the supervision and direct command of a Range Officer competitors must carry their handguns unloaded in a gun case, gun bag or in a holster on a belt worn by the competitor. A competitor who, while not at a safety area, staging area, or under RO supervision, removes their holster or their equipment belt with their handgun still in the holster, shall be considered to be in violation of this rule and subject to disqualification from the match. Handguns removed in this fashion in a staging area may not be removed from the holster in the staging area.

5.2.1.2   Competitors carrying their handgun in a holster must have an empty magazine well and the hammer or striker must be de-cocked. Anyone found in violation of this rule will be immediately escorted by a Range Officer to a suitable range or safety area where appropriate corrective action shall be made.

5.2.1.3   The belt carrying the holster must be worn at waist level which is deemed to be at the same level as the original belt loops on the lower garment. The belt or the inner belt (or both) must be either securely fixed at the waist. Thigh holsters and mag holders are specifically allowed. Female competitors may be permitted to wear a belt at hip level however; the top of the belt must not be positioned below the furthest lateral point of the top of the femur (tuberosity major).

5.2.1.3.1 The holster must be capable of retaining the handgun during the vigorous movement that may be required during the courses of fire.

5.2.1.3.2 The holster must allow the competitor to safely draw and re-holster the handgun without causing the muzzle to point in an unsafe direction.

5.2.1.3.3 The holster must completely prevent access to, or activation of the trigger of the handgun while holstered.

5.2.1.3.4 The Range Master may deem that a competitor's holster is unsafe and order that it be improved to his satisfaction, failing which it must be withdrawn from the match.

5.2.1.4 Competitors deemed by the Range Master to be significantly disabled may be given special dispensation in relation to the type and/or placement of their holster and related equipment and the Range Master will remain the final authority in respect of the safety and suitability of using such equipment at USPSA matches.

5.2.2 **Long guns (Includes PCC)**

5.2.2.1 Except when within the boundaries of a safety area, or when under the supervision and direct command of a Range Officer, competitors must carry their long guns:

5.2.2.1.1 With detachable magazines removed.

5.2.2.1.2 Competitors must use a chamber safety flag, or clear chamber device, that is easily visible externally to the gun when transporting from vehicles or stage to stage. Anyone found in violation of this rule will be immediately escorted by a Range Officer to a suitable range or safety area where appropriate corrective action shall be made.

5.2.2.1.3 Unbagged long guns must be carried, shouldered or slung from the shoulder with the firearm reasonably vertical. Match Directors may require this to be "vertically upwards" or "vertically downwards" providing this is made clear to all competitors in a reasonable manner.

5.2.2.1.4 When transporting non-preloaded long guns from the staging area to the start position and back from where the shooter unloads and shows clear, the gun must be carried muzzle vertically upwards with the bolt closed on a chamber safety flag.

5.2.2.1.5 Transporting a preloaded shotgun from the preload table to the start position the firearm must be carried directly to the start position with the muzzle vertically upwards and the bolt closed on a chamber safety flag.

5.2.3 Belts, holsters, belt-mounted magazine holders and speed-loading devices and any other equipment worn or carried by the shooter may be changed, repositioned or reconfigured between stages provided that all equipment is in a rules-compliant configuration prior to the start of the shooter's attempt on the Course of Fire.

5.2.4 Firearms that are being transported on a cart, vehicle, or other such conveyance must be situated on the conveyance in either a muzzle up or muzzle down orientation if not bagged. Under such conditions long guns must have a chamber safety flag inserted. The muzzle of any such firearm, if oriented down, must point to a spot within 3 feet of the conveyance. If pointed up, it must be oriented such that a person walking around the conveyance will not be covered by the muzzle if they are more than 3 feet away from the conveyance. All such measurements shall be taken while the conveyance is situated on flat, level ground. In the event of disagreement on how the firearm is being transported, the Range Master shall be the final authority as to the acceptability of such orientation.

5.2.4.1 Long guns (Rifles, Shotguns, and PCCs) must be cased/uncased or removed/replaced on a cart with the muzzle pointed in a safe direction, as described above, directly into and within 2 yards of a side berm or backstop. Long guns can also be cased/uncased or removed/replaced on a cart under the direct supervision of a range officer with muzzle pointing at the backstop. Failure to point the muzzle at a side berm or back stop during casing/uncasing or removing/replacing on a cart will result in a DQ per 10.5.20. (Note: 2.4.1 prohibits handguns from being handled in this fashion. Handguns may only be handled in a Safety Area.)

5.3 Appropriate Dress

5.3.1 The use of offensive or objectionable garments is not allowed. The Match Director will have final authority regarding what garments competitors are allowed to wear.

5.4 Eye and Hearing Protection

5.4.1 All persons near an area potentially exposed to ricochet debris or bullet fragments are required to wear eye protection. All persons near an area where the sound of firearms being fired may potentially cause hearing damage are required to wear or use adequate hearing protection.

5.4.2   If a Range Officer deems that a competitor about to attempt a course of fire is wearing inadequate eye or hearing protection, the Range Officer may order the competitor to rectify the situation before allowing the competitor to continue. The Range Master is the final authority on this matter.

5.4.3   If a Range Official notices that a competitor has lost or displaced their eye or hearing protection during a course of fire, or has commenced a course of fire without them, the Range Official must immediately stop the competitor who will be required to reshoot the course of fire after the protective devices have been restored.

5.4.4   A competitor who inadvertently loses eye or hearing protection during a course of fire, or commences a course of fire without them, is entitled to stop, point their firearm in a safe direction and indicate the problem to the Range Official, in which case the provisions of the previous rule will apply.

5.4.5   A competitor who intentionally loses or displaces eye and/or hearing protection during a course of fire will be disallowed the provisions of Rule 5.4.4 and will be subject to match disqualification. (See Rule 10.6.3.)

5.5   Ammunition and Related Equipment

5.5.1   Unless specifically prohibited in the Written Stage Briefing, spare ammunition, magazines and/or speed loading devices must be carried anywhere on the shooter's person or firearm. The shooter must not be allowed to have ammunition or magazines/speed loading devices in their hands at the start signal.

5.5.2   Magazines and speed loading devices must comply with the provisions of the relevant Division. Detachable magazines are defined as speed loaders. For any Division where speed loaders are not allowed this will apply to detachable magazines as well.

5.5.3   Spare magazines, speed loading devices or ammunition dropped or discarded by a competitor after the start signal may be retrieved; however, their retrieval is at all times subject to all safety rules.

5.5.4   Shotgun speed loaders (Tec Loaders) must have the primer relief cut.

5.5.5   Metal piercing, steel core or jacketed, incendiary and/or tracer ammunition is prohibited at USPSA matches. (See Rule 10.5.14.) Steel and/or tungsten shot, or slugs may not be used. For shotgun ammo, the Match Director and/or Range Master may restrict ammunition to certain minimum and/or maximum shot sizes or types for reasons of safety.

5.5.6   All ammunition used by a competitor must satisfy the requirements of the relevant Division.

5.5.7   Any ammunition deemed unsafe by a Range Officer must be immediately withdrawn from the match.

5.5.8   Ammunition (other than shot shells loaded with birdshot or buckshot) must not discharge more than one bullet or other scoring projectile from a single round.

5.5.9   Competitors at an USPSA match are solely and personally responsible for the safety of all and any ammunition which they bring to the match. Neither USPSA nor any USPSA Officers, nor any organization affiliated to USPSA, or the officers of any organization affiliated to USPSA accepts any responsibility whatsoever in this regard, nor in respect of any loss, damage, accident, injury or death suffered by any person or entity as a result of the lawful or unlawful use of any such ammunition.

5.6   Chronograph and Power Factors

5.6.1   One or more official match chronographs are used to assist in the determination of the power factor of every competitor's ammunition. In the absence of official match chronograph(s), the power factor declared by a competitor cannot be challenged.

   5.6.1.1   The power factor rating to enable a competitor's scores to be included in match results is called "Minor". Some Divisions offer a higher power factor rating called "Major", which enables competitors to earn more points for peripheral shots on scoring cardboard targets.

   5.6.1.2   The power factor floor for Minor rating and the power factor floor for Major rating, if available, and other specific requirements applicable to each Division are stipulated in Appendices D1 to D5.

   5.6.1.3   The associated values awarded for Minor and Major scoring hits are illustrated in Appendix B1.

   5.6.1.4   The method used to determine power factor and the procedures used at the Chronograph Station are stipulated in Appendix C2.

5.7   Malfunctions of Competitor's Equipment

5.7.1   A competitor who experiences a malfunction while responding to the "Make Ready" command, but prior to issuance of the "Start Signal" is entitled to retire to repair his firearm without penalty, under the authority and supervision of the officiating Range Officer and subject to all other safety rules. Once the repairs have been completed or a replacement firearm has been approved by the Range Master, the competitor may return to attempt the course of fire, subject to scheduling as determined by the officiating Range Officer or Range Master.

5.7.2   In the event that a competitor's firearm malfunctions after the Start signal the competitor may safely attempt to correct the problem and continue the course of fire. During such corrective action the competitor must keep his firearm's muzzle pointing safely downrange at all times.

5.7.3 While rectifying a malfunction, the competitor's fingers must be clearly visible outside the trigger guard. (See Rule 10.5.7)

5.7.4 In the event that a malfunction cannot be corrected by the competitor within 2 minutes he must point the firearm safely downrange and advise the Range Officer who will terminate the course of fire in the normal manner. The course of fire will be scored as shot including all applicable misses and penalties.

5.7.5 Under no circumstances is a competitor permitted to leave a course of fire in the possession of a loaded firearm. (See Rule 10.5.12.)

5.7.6 Where the firearm has failed after the Start signal the competitor must not be permitted to reshoot the course of fire or string. This includes the instance where a firearm is declared unserviceable or unsafe during a course of fire. However, any un-attempted component strings in a Standard Exercise may still be attempted by the affected competitor after the firearm has been repaired, and prior to when match results are declared final by the Match Director.

5.7.7 In the event that a Range Officer terminates a course of fire due to a suspicion that a competitor has an unsafe firearm or unsafe ammunition (e.g., a "squib" load) the Range Officer will take whatever steps he deems necessary to return both the competitor and the range to a safe condition. The Range Officer will then inspect the firearm or ammunition and proceed as follows:

5.7.7.1 If the Range Officer finds evidence that confirms the suspected problem the competitor will not be entitled to a reshoot but will be ordered to rectify the problem. On the competitor's score sheet the time will be recorded up to the last shot fired and the course of fire will be scored "as shot" including all applicable misses and penalties.

5.7.7.2 If the Range Officer discovers that the suspected safety problem does not exist, the competitor will be required to reshoot the stage.

5.7.7.3 A competitor who suspects a "squib" but was not stopped by the range officer is allowed to safely abandon the firearm and finish the stage unless it was the final firearm. In that case the time will be recorded, and the stage will be scored as normal. However, any attempt to clear a suspected "squib" is specifically prohibited under this provision whether the range officer has previously called stop or not.

5.8 Certified Ammunition

Use of Certified Ammunition is subject to the conditions and constraints in <u>Appendix C3</u>. Failure to comply with the conditions and constraints voids the competitor's inclusion in the Certified Ammunition Program for that match.   *NOTE: Applies to Hit Factor Scoring only.

CHAPTER 6 – Match Structure

6.1 General Principles

The following definitions are used for clarity:

6.1.1 **Stage** – A separately timed and scored component of a match.

6.1.2 **Match** – Consists of a minimum of 2 stages. The total sum of individual stage results will be accumulated to declare a match winner.

6.1.3 **Tournament** – Consists of two or more firearm specific matches (e.g. a handgun match and a shotgun match, or a handgun match, a rifle match and a shotgun match), or two or more handgun-type matches (e.g. a 1911 handgun match and a "Brand A" handgun match). The individual match results achieved by a competitor in each component match will be used to declare an overall tournament winner.

6.1.4 **League** – Consists of two or more USPSA matches held at different locations and on different dates. The total sum of match results attained by each competitor at component matches specified by the league organizers will be accumulated to determine a league winner.

6.1.5 **Shoot-Off** – An event conducted separately from a match. Eligible competitors compete directly against each other by simultaneously shooting at separate but equal target arrays in a process of elimination.

6.2 Match Divisions

6.2.1 USPSA Divisions recognize different firearms and equipment. (See Appendices D1 to D5.) Each match must recognize at least one Division. When multiple Divisions are available in a match each Division must be scored separately and independently and match results must recognize a winner in each Division.

6.2.2 In USPSA sanctioned matches, the minimum number of competitors stipulated in Appendix A2 must compete in each Division for it to be recognized. If there are insufficient competitors in a Division, the Match Director may allow that Division to stand without official USPSA recognition.

6.2.3 Prior to the commencement of a match each competitor must declare one Division for score. Match Officials should check firearms and other competitor equipment for compliance with the declared Division prior to the competitor making an attempt at any of the courses of fire.

6.2.4 Subject to the prior approval of the Match Director, a competitor may enter a match in more than one Division. However, the competitor may compete for match score in only one Division and that must be the first attempt in all cases. Any subsequent attempts in another Division will not count for match recognition.

6.2.4.1   Level I matches may allow competitors to enter multiple Divisions for match recognition.

6.2.5   Where a Division is unavailable or deleted, or where a competitor fails to declare a specific Division prior to the commencement of a match, the competitor will be placed in the Division which, in the opinion of the Range Master, most closely identifies with the competitor's equipment. If, in the opinion of the Range Master, no suitable Division is available the competitor will shoot the match for no score.

6.2.5.1   If a competitor fails to satisfy the equipment or other requirements of a declared Division during a course of fire the competitor will be placed in Open Division, if available. If a competitor fails to satisfy the equipment or other requirements for Open Division during the course of fire, he will shoot for no score.

6.2.5.2   A competitor who is classified or reclassified as above must be notified as soon as possible. The Range Master's decision on these matters is final.

6.2.6   A match disqualification incurred by a competitor at any time during a match will prevent the competitor from further participation in the match including any subsequent attempts in another Division. However, this is not retroactive. Any previous and complete match scores from another Division will be included for recognition and awards in that Division.

6.2.7   Recognition of a competitor in a specific Division will not preclude further recognition in a Category.

6.3   Match Categories

6.3.1   USPSA matches may include different Categories within each Division to recognize different groups of competitors. A competitor may declare multiple Categories for a match or tournament.

6.3.2   Failure to meet the requirements of the declared Categories or failure to declare a Category prior to the start of the match will result in exclusion from that Category. Details of currently approved Categories and related requirements are listed in Appendix A2.

6.4   Competitor Status and Credentials

6.4.1   All competitors must be individual members of USPSA or a current member of their IPSC region for Level II and above competitions. A competitor who submits a paid USPSA membership application to the Match Director or presents proof of online registration and payment as a new member prior to entering the competition is considered a member for the purpose of this rule.

6.4.1.1   Anyone whose membership has been suspended or terminated by USPSA will no longer be eligible to compete in any USPSA match including local (level I) matches. A list of those who are ineligible will be kept at USPSA headquarters for verification.

6.4.2   USPSA Competition Match classifications do not apply to rifle, shotgun, or multigun and will not be used in USPSA rifle, shotgun, or multigun matches.

6.4.3   No person may be barred from participating in a USPSA match based on gender, race, religion or occupation.

6.4.4   An individual may be barred from participating in a USPSA match, at the match director's discretion, if the person:

6.4.4.1   has demonstrated an inability to safely complete courses of fire, or

6.4.4.2   has demonstrated behavior which would or may disrupt the match, or which would bring disrepute to the sport.

6.4.5   A Match Director enforcing Rule 6.4.4 must submit a detailed report to USPSA within seven days of the occurrence. Rule 6.4.4 applies to single matches only. Each match in which an individual is barred must be properly documented as above.

6.5   Competitor Scheduling and Squadding

6.5.1   Competitors must compete for score according to the published match and squadding schedule. A competitor who is not present at the scheduled time and date for any stage may not attempt that stage without the prior approval of the Match Director or Range Master, failing which the competitor's score for that stage will be zero.

6.5.2   Range Officials, match sponsors and other persons may compete for score in a "pre-match," subject to the prior approval of the Match Director. Competitors in the main match must not be restricted from viewing the pre-match. Scores attained in the "pre-match" may, at the discretion of the Match Director, be included in the overall match results provided the dates of the "pre-match" are published in the official match schedule.

6.5.3   A match, tournament or league will be deemed to have started on the first day that competitors (including those specified above) shoot for score and will be deemed to have ended when the results have been declared final by the Match Director.

CHAPTER 7 – Match Management

7.1 Match Officials

The duties and terms of reference of Match Officials are defined as follows:

7.1.1   **Range Officer** ("RO") – issues range commands, oversees competitor compliance with the written stage briefing and closely monitors safe competitor action. He also declares the time, scores, and penalties achieved by each competitor and verifies that these are correctly recorded on the competitor's score sheet (under the authority of a Chief Range Officer and Range Master).

7.1.2   **Chief Range Officer** ("CRO") – is the primary authority over all persons and activities in the courses of fire under his control, and oversees the fair, correct and consistent application of these rules (under the authority of the Range Master).

7.1.3   **Chrono Officer** ("CO") – is the primary authority over all persons and activities at the Chronograph Station, and oversees the fair, correct and consistent application of the pertinent rules and the procedures outlined in Appendix C2 (under direct authority of the Range Master).

7.1.4   **Stats Officer** ("SO") – collects, sorts, verifies, tabulates and retains all score sheets and ultimately produces provisional and final results (under direct authority of the Range Master.) Any incomplete or inaccurate score sheets must be promptly referred to the Range Master.

7.1.5   **Quartermaster** ("QM") – distributes, repairs and maintains all range equipment and supplies (e.g., targets, patches, paint, props, timers, batteries, staplers, clipboards etc.) (under direct authority of the Range Master).

7.1.6   **Range Master** ("RM") – has overall authority over all persons and activities within the entire range, including range safety, the operation of all courses of fire and the application of these rules. All match disqualifications and appeals to arbitration must be brought to his attention. The Range Master is usually appointed by and works with the Match Director. However, in respect of USPSA sanctioned Level III and Nationals matches, the appointment of the Range Master is subject to the prior written approval of the Director of NROI.

7.1.7   **Match Director** ("MD") – handles overall match administration including squadding, scheduling, range construction, the coordination of all support staff and the provision of services. His authority and decisions will prevail with regard to all matters except in respect of matters in these rules which are the domain of the Range Master. The Match Director is appointed by the host organization and works with the Range Master.

7.1.8   **Director NROI** ("DNROI") - While serving at a match as a member of the staff carries the same overall authority as the Match Director and Range Master. The DNROI while on staff will be there to assist the Match Director and Range Master in all endeavors to keep things running smoothly and help to make the match a success.

7.2 Discipline of Match Officials

7.2.1 The Range Master has authority over all Match Officials other than the Match Director (except when the Match Director is actually participating as a competitor at the match,) and is responsible for decisions in matters concerning conduct and discipline.

7.2.2 In the event that a Match Official is disciplined the Range Master must send a report of the incident and details of the disciplinary action to the Director of NROI.

7.2.3 A Match Official who is disqualified from a match for a safety infraction while competing will continue to be eligible to serve as a Match Official for the match, providing the medical provisions in 10.3.1 are not the cause of the disqualification. The Range Master will make all decisions related to an official's participation if the official is disqualified for any reason other than a safety violation.

7.2.4 All match officials are subject to the current published Range Officer Discipline Policy, which is posted on the USPSA web site.

7.3 Appointment of Officials

7.3.1 Match organizers must, prior to commencement of a match, appoint a Match Director and a Range Master to carry out the duties detailed in these rules. The nominated Range Master should preferably be the most competent and experienced certified Range Official present. (See Rule 7.1.6.) For Level I and Level II matches a single person may be appointed to be both the Match Director and the Range Master.

7.3.2 References in these rules to Range Officials (e.g., "Range Officer," "Range Master," etc.) mean personnel who have been officially appointed by match organizers to actually serve in an official capacity at the match. Persons who are certified Range Officials but who are actually participating in the match as regular competitors have no standing or authority as Range Officials for that match. Such persons should therefore not participate in the match wearing garments bearing NROI insignia.

7.3.3 Matches of all Levels shall publicly publish or announce to competitors the identity of the Match Director, Range Master, Stats Officer or other match officials as appropriate to the level of match.

CHAPTER 8 – The Course of Fire

8.1 Firearm Ready Conditions

The ready condition for firearms will normally be as stated below. Note that a course of fire may require that a firearm be "staged" (prepared and placed prior to the start signal in a specific position and condition for use later during the course of fire). In such cases the written course description must define the position, condition and location of the staged firearm(s). However, in the event that a competitor fails to load the chamber when permitted by the written stage briefing, whether inadvertently or intentionally, the Range Officer must not take any action, as the competitor is always responsible for the handling of the firearm.

8.1.1 Revolvers:

8.1.1.1 Single Action – hammer fully down on an empty chamber or, if a safety notch is fitted, hammer down over a loaded chamber (transfer bar designs excepted).

8.1.1.2 Double Action – hammer fully down and all chambers may be loaded.

8.1.2 Autoloaders (treat all Rifles, Shotguns, and PCCs as "Single Action"):

8.1.2.1 **"Single action"** – chamber loaded, hammer cocked, and the safety fully engaged (if the firearm is designed to have one). For all guns, the safety must remain on until the start signal. Empty chamber, magazine inserted, and hammer fully down do not have to have the primary (thumb) safety engaged, as it is not possible in most cases to engage the safety or actuate the trigger or hammer. If the primary safety can be applied in this condition, then it must still be applied.

Note: Placing the safety on a loaded long gun into the off position after it has been placed in the on position between assuming the start position and the start signal is prohibited. A shooter who prematurely disengages the safety must be restarted for being in an improper start position/condition.

8.1.2.2 **"Double action"** – chamber loaded, hammer fully down or de-cocked.

8.1.2.3 **"Selective action"** – chamber loaded with hammer fully down, or chamber loaded, and hammer cocked with external safety fully engaged.

8.1.2.4 With respect to Rules 8.1.2.1 and 8.1.2.3 the term "safety" means the primary visible safety lever on the firearm (e.g., the thumb safety on a "1911" genre handgun in order to be in compliance with 10.5.10, except as noted in 8.1.2.1.

8.1.2.5　When applicable, the grip safety may be disabled provided that the primary safety as described in <u>8.1.2.4</u> is operable.

8.1.3　Courses of fire may require ready conditions which are different to those stated above. If the firearm is to be prepared with an empty chamber (or cylinder) the action must be fully forward and closed (or the cylinder must be fully closed) and the hammer or striker must be fully down or fully forward, as the case may be, unless otherwise specified in the stage briefing.

8.1.4　Unless complying with a Division requirement (see Appendices), a competitor must not be restricted on the number of rounds to be loaded or reloaded. Written stage briefings may only stipulate when the firearm is to be loaded or when mandatory reloads are required.

8.1.4.1　Exception: A Speed shoot or Standard Exercises type stage may specify the number of rounds on a shotgun reload.

8.1.5　For handguns used at USPSA matches the following definitions apply:

8.1.5.1　"**Single Action**" means activation of the trigger causes a single action to occur (i.e., the hammer or striker falls).

8.1.5.2　"**Double Action**" means activation of the trigger causes more than a single action to occur (i.e., the hammer or striker rises or retracts, then falls).

8.1.5.3　"**Striker Fired**" means activation of the trigger, once the chamber of the firearm is loaded, finishes cocking the striker spring and then causes the striker to fall.

8.1.5.4　"**Selective Action**" means that the handgun can be operated in either "Single Action" or "Double Action" modes.

8.2　Competitor Ready Condition

8.2.1　The firearm is prepared as specified in the written stage briefing, and is in compliance with the requirements of the relevant Division.

8.2.2　The competitor assumes the start position as specified in the written stage briefing.

8.2.3　A competitor who attempts or completes a course of fire where an incorrect start position was used must be required by a Range Official to reshoot the course of fire.

8.2.4　A course of fire must never require or allow a competitor to touch or hold a handgun, or any loading device or ammunition after the "Standby" command and before the "Start Signal" (except for unavoidable touching with the lower arms).

8.2.5　A course of fire must never require the competitor to draw a handgun from the holster with the weak hand. A course of fire must never require a competitor to start with a long gun held on the weak side, and stage briefings may never require a long gun to be fired using only one hand.

8.2.6   A course of fire must never require the competitor to re-holster a handgun after the start signal. However, a competitor may re-holster provided this is accomplished safely and the handgun is either unloaded or in a ready condition stated in Section 8.1.

8.2.7   In a course of fire that requires a slung long gun be carried during a stage the chamber must be empty and the shooter is not subject to disqualification under Rule 10.5.2 while the long gun is slung. This exemption from 10.5.2 ends when the shooter first starts to manipulate the action of the firearm to chamber a round.

8.3   Range Communication

The approved range commands and their sequence are as follows:

8.3.1   **"Make Ready"** – This command signifies the start of "the Course of Fire." Under the direct supervision of the Range Officer the competitor must face downrange, or in a safe direction as specified by the Range Officer, fit eye and ear protection, and prepare the firearm(s) in accordance with the written stage briefing. The competitor must then assume the required start position. The Range Officer will not proceed with any further range commands until the competitor is still and is in the correct start position.

8.3.1.1   The initial "Make Ready" command defines the start of the "Course of Fire" regardless of how many firearms are subsequently prepared, loaded and/or staged following that command.

8.3.1.2   Where more than one firearm will be used during a course of fire the Range Officer will direct and supervise the competitor through the process of preparing all firearms. This may include verbal instructions.

8.3.1.3   A shotgun pre-loading area may be used on any stage subject to the Range Master's discretion and may also be used as a staging area. The pre-loading area must be in a safe position and orientation, outside the active stage boundaries but still well within the confines of the berm or in a controlled area for stages outside of regular berms. It must be clearly and obviously marked to distinguish it from a Safety Area.

8.3.1.4   Shotgun pre-loading activity begins with a pre-Load directive from the supervising Range Officer. Competitors may pre-load in the shotgun pre-loading area only under the active direction and supervision of a Range Officer. The entire squad can be pre-loaded at once to save time. All pre-loading activity, including transporting loaded guns to start position(s), is subject to the provisions of relevant safety regulations including (but not limited to) the following Rules: 10.4.3 (shot while loading), 10.5.1 (handling firearm without RO supervision), 10.5.2 (unsafe muzzle direction), 10.5.3 (dropped gun), 10.5.8 (finger inside trigger guard during loading), etc. Pre-loading a shotgun without direction and active supervision by a range officer will cause the competitor to be disqualified for unsafe gun handling per Rule 10.5.1.

8.3.1.4.1   Only the tube will be pre-loaded. A shooter arriving at the line with a preloaded shotgun that is found to have a round in the chamber will be subject to disqualification under Rule 10.5.12. If the competitor should accidentally or inadvertently chamber a round during the preload, the Range Officer shall take such action as is necessary to have the competitor correct the error. However, if the competitor, for whatever reason, should arrive at the line with a round in the chamber, the preceding shall not be allowed as a defense against disqualification under 10.5.12.

8.3.1.5   Once the Make Ready command has been given, the competitor must not move away from the start location prior to issuance of the Start Signal without the prior approval, and under the direct supervision of the Range Officer. (See Rule 8.7.1.)

8.3.1.6   Sight pictures may be taken during the Make Ready process and while preparing for the next string. Should the competitor experience an accidental discharge while taking a sight picture a disqualification under rule 10.4.3 shall be issued.

8.3.2   **"Are You Ready?"** – The lack of any negative response from the competitor indicates that he fully understands the requirements of the course of fire and is ready to proceed. If the competitor is not ready at the Are You Ready? command, he must state "Not Ready." It is suggested that when the competitor is ready, he should assume the required start position to indicate his readiness to the Range Officer.

8.3.3   **"Standby"** – This command should be followed by the start signal within 1 to 4 seconds.

8.3.4   **"Start Signal"** – The signal for the competitor to begin their attempt at the course of fire. If a competitor fails to react to an audible start signal, for any reason, the Range Officer will confirm that the competitor is ready to attempt the course of fire, and will resume the range commands from "Are You Ready?"

8.3.4.1 In the event that a competitor begins his attempt at the course of fire prematurely ("false start" prior to the issuance of the start signal) the Range Officer will, as soon as possible, stop and restart the competitor once the course of fire has been restored.

8.3.5 **"Stop"** – Any Range Officer assigned to a stage may issue this command at any time during the course of fire. The competitor must immediately cease firing, stop moving and wait for further instructions from the Range Officer.

8.3.6 **"If You Are Finished, Unload and Show Clear"** or **"Unload and Show Clear"** – If the competitor has finished shooting, he must lower his firearm and present it for inspection by the Range Officer with the muzzle pointed downrange, fixed magazine empty, detachable magazine removed, action locked or held open, and chamber empty. Revolvers must be presented with the cylinder swung out and empty. Where more than one firearm is used during a course of fire, the Range Officer will supervise the shooter through the procedure for clearing each firearm in turn. Only when ALL firearms have been cleared will the Range Officer declare "Range Is Clear."

8.3.7 **"If Clear, Hammer Down, Holster"** or **"If Clear, Hammer Down, Flag"** – After issuance of this command, the competitor is prohibited from firing. (See Rule 10.4.3.) While continuing to point the firearm safely downrange, the competitor must perform a final safety check as follows:

8.3.7.1 Self-loaders, also including manual action rifles and shotguns – point the firearm downrange, release the slide or close the bolt and pull the trigger without touching the hammer or decocker, if any. For PCCs, rifles and shotguns, pull the trigger, then re-open the action, lock it open and apply safety catches (if possible). The action will be closed on a chamber flag.

8.3.7.2 Revolvers – close the empty cylinder without touching the hammer, if any.

8.3.7.3 If the gun proves to be clear, the competitor must holster his handgun, and carry his PCC, rifle or shotgun vertically muzzle up or down.

8.3.7.4 If the gun does not prove to be clear, the Range Officer will issue the stop command, (8.3.5), order the competitor to unload and show clear, (8.3.6), and complete the range commands in 8.3.7 and 8.3.8. The competitor will then be disqualified under 10.4.3.

8.3.8 **"Range Is Clear"** – This declaration signifies the end of the Course of fire. Once the declaration is made officials and competitors may move forward to score, patch, reset targets, etc.

8.4 Loading, Reloading, Unloading, or Abandoning a Firearm During a Course of Fire

8.4.1 When loading, reloading or unloading during a course of fire, the competitor's fingers must be visibly outside the trigger guard and the firearm must be pointed safely downrange or in another safe direction authorized by a Range Officer. (See Rules 10.5.2 and 10.5.8.)

8.4.2 Within the context of a Multigun stage a competitor may be required to "abandon" a firearm in order to use another firearm. In this context an "abandoned firearm" is a firearm which the competitor has used, placed in the provided retention device in accordance with course requirements, and subsequently moved more than one (1) yard away from. A competitor may return to and use an abandoned firearm provided its retrieval and use is done safely and in accordance with the stage procedure and all subsequent rules in this section. RO's are cautioned about clearing abandoned firearms prematurely. (See Rule 8.4.2.3.)

8.4.2.1 An abandoned firearm must be in applicable ready condition (Section 8.1) or empty with no ammunition anywhere in the firearm. (See Rule 10.2.13.)

8.4.2.2 A competitor may, during abandonment of one firearm, handle another firearm to be used without penalty, providing all safety aspects are followed. (e.g., Abandoning a shotgun, and a handgun is to be used for the next array of targets, the competitor may draw the handgun while in the act of abandoning the shotgun). Neither firearm may be fired while competitor has both in hand. (See Rule 10.2.10.)

8.4.2.3 In order to reduce stage clearance time a Range Officer may be assigned to clear "abandoned" firearms, at the Range Master's discretion, provided the stage design allows for this to be done in a way that allows the gun to be cleared in a safe direction and without interfering with the competitor's attempt at the course of fire. In such cases the competitor's delegate will accompany the official responsible for clearing abandoned firearms. Competitors must be advised of this procedure during the stage briefing. The RO and delegate shall verify that the abandoned firearm is in a legal abandoned state (e.g., properly positioned and safety-on or firearm empty). Upon verifying the condition, the RO will clear the firearm with the delegate confirming it is clear. The firearm may then be transported to the staging area or other specified location behind the firing line. Handguns must be bagged if they are to be moved to the staging area or a safe area. The Range Officer is responsible for the safe handling of the firearm during this process, including (but not limited to) muzzle direction.

8.5 Movement

8.5.1 Except when the competitor is actually aiming or shooting at targets all movement (see Glossary, App. A3) must be accomplished with the fingers visibly outside the trigger guard.

8.5.2   If a competitor holsters a loaded handgun at any time during a course of fire it must be placed in the applicable handgun ready conditions. (See Section 8.1.) Violations will be subject to match disqualification. (See Rule 10.5.10.) The re-slinging of a rifle or PCC during a course of fire is prohibited. (See Rule 10.5.17.)

8.5.2.1   For a single action self-loader the safety must be applied.

8.5.2.2   For double action self-loaders and revolvers the hammer must be down, or, if present, the safety applied if the hammer is cocked.

8.6   Assistance or Interference

8.6.1   No assistance of any kind can be given to a competitor during a course of fire, except that any Range Officer assigned to a stage may issue safety warnings to a competitor at any time. Such warnings will not be grounds for the competitor to be awarded a reshoot.

8.6.2   Any person providing interference or unauthorized assistance to a competitor during a course of fire (and the competitor receiving such assistance) may, at the discretion of a Range Officer, incur a procedural penalty for that stage and/or be subject to Section 10.6.

8.6.2.1   When approved by the Range Officer, competitors at Level I matches may, without penalty, receive whatever coaching or assistance they request. Range Officials may safety coach competitors as needed, unless a safety violation occurs.

8.6.3   Competitors confined to wheelchairs or similar devices may be given special dispensation by the Range Master in respect of mobility assistance; however, the provisions of Rule 10.2.11 may still apply at the Range Master's discretion.

8.6.4   In the event that inadvertent contact from the Range Officer or another external influence has interfered with the competitor during a course of fire, the Range Officer may offer the competitor a reshoot of the course of fire. The competitor must accept or decline the offer prior to seeing either the time or the score from the initial attempt. However, in the event that the competitor commits a safety infraction during any such interference, the provisions of Section 10.3 may still apply.

8.6.5   Calling hits on self-indicating targets or fixed metal targets by range officials is allowed and not considered interference or coaching. If range officials call a hit in error, when an actual miss occurred, the call of "hit" will stand and is not reason for a reshoot, nor subject to appeal.

8.7   Sight Pictures and Range Inspection

8.7.1   A competitor is permitted to take a sight picture prior to the start signal. Such sight picture is only permitted from the "Make Ready" location. On a multigun stage sight pictures are permitted for each firearm, but only from the staged/make ready locations. For a rifle stage the competitor may move within reason to a location that allows a sight picture on the actual targets.

8.7.2   Competitors are prohibited from using any guns or gun replicas as sighting aids while conducting their inspection ("walkthrough") of a course of fire. Violations will incur one procedural penalty per occurrence. (See also Rule 10.5.1.)

8.7.3   No person is permitted to enter or move through a course of fire without the prior approval of a Range Officer assigned to that course of fire or the Range Master.

8.7.4   A course of fire is considered closed or off limits when there are no official match staff present to supervise competitor actions during stage inspection. Normal stage inspection is allowed during the hours of the match, providing there are match staff present or the match director has specifically approved inspection of courses with no match staff present. Reasonable attempts must be made to communicate information about closed courses to all competitors (such as but not limited to publishing in the match book, group emails, posting signage, etc.).

8.7.4.1   Altering stage props, targets or any other part of a COF without the approval of a Range Officer, or setting, resetting or activating moving targets on a COF identified as "Closed" or "Off Limits" will be subject to the provisions of Section 10.6.

8.7.5   Any person interfering with the scoring or resetting of a course of fire in any way may be assessed a procedural penalty or be subject to the provisions of 10.6. The Range Master shall be called in all cases and will make the decision as to what penalty to assess.

CHAPTER 9 – Scoring

Scoring Methods: There are two approved scoring systems for USPSA Rifle, Shotgun, or Multigun matches, Traditional USPSA Hit Factor Scoring and Time Plus. Either system may be used for 2-Gun (Pistol/PCC or Pistol/Rifle), or Rifle or Shotgun only matches. However, Multigun (all three or four guns) matches must be scored using Time Plus. If Hit Factor scoring is used for 2-Gun matches, all firearms will be scored using minor power factor values.

9.1   General Regulations that apply to both scoring systems:

9.1.1   Approaching Targets – While scoring is in progress, competitors or their delegate must not approach any target closer than 3 feet without the authorization of the Range Officer. Violation may, at the discretion of the Range Officer, incur a procedural penalty.

9.1.2   Touching Targets – While scoring is in progress competitors or their delegate must not touch, gauge or otherwise interfere with any target without the authorization of the Range Officer. Should a Range Officer deem that a competitor or their delegate has influenced or affected the scoring process due to such interference the Range Officer may:

9.1.2.1   Score the affected target as a missed target; or

9.1.2.2   Impose penalties for any affected no-shoots.

9.1.3   Prematurely Patched Targets – If a target is prematurely patched or taped, which prevents a Range Official from determining the actual score, the Range Officer must order the competitor to reshoot the course of fire. However, if following the scoring of a target by any assigned Range Officer, the target is patched or taped by anyone other than a Range Officer, the score will stand as called regardless of the competitor's opportunity to see the target in question and the competitor will not be permitted to appeal the score as called. Reviewing previous score sheets is prohibited; targets must be scored as is, using the actual target as the basis for the scoring call.

9.1.4   Unrestored Targets – If, following completion of a course of fire by a previous competitor, one or more targets have not been properly patched or taped or if previously applied pasters have fallen off the target for the competitor being scored the Range Officer must judge whether or not an accurate score can be determined. If there are extra scoring hits or questionable penalty hits thereon and it is not obvious which hits were made by the competitor being scored the affected competitor must be ordered to reshoot the course of fire. Reviewing previous score sheets is prohibited. Targets must be scored as is using the actual target as the basis for the scoring call.

9.1.5   Impenetrable – The scoring area of USPSA scoring targets and no-shoots is deemed to be impenetrable:

9.1.5.1   If a bullet or slug strikes wholly within the scoring area of a cardboard target and continues on to strike the scoring area of another cardboard target the hit on the subsequent cardboard target will not count for score or penalty, as the case may be. If it cannot be determined which hit(s) struck wholly within a cardboard target and subsequently struck another cardboard target, a reshoot shall be ordered.

9.1.5.1.1   In accordance with Rule 9.1.5, the scoring areas of scoring targets and no-shoots are impenetrable. Whenever two targets (scoring and/or no-shoots) are in direct contact where one target directly overlaps part of another target, the area of the "under" target which is directly covered by the scoring area of the "over" target and its perforations is deemed to be non-existent.

9.1.5.2   If a bullet or slug strikes wholly within the scoring area of a cardboard target and continues on to hit a plate or strike down a popper it will be treated as range equipment failure. The competitor will be required to reshoot the course of fire after it has been restored.

9.1.5.3   If a bullet or slug strikes partially within the scoring area of a cardboard or metal target and continues on to strike the scoring area of another cardboard target the hit on the subsequent cardboard target will also count for score or penalty, as the case may be.

9.1.5.4   If a bullet or slug strikes partially within the scoring area of a cardboard or metal target and continues on to strike down or hit the scoring area of another metal target the subsequent metal target will also count for score or penalty, as the case may be.

9.1.6   Unless specifically described as "soft cover" in the written stage briefing, all props, walls, barriers, vision screens and other obstacles are deemed to be impenetrable "hard cover":

9.1.6.1   If a bullet or slug strikes wholly within hard cover and continues on to strike any scoring cardboard target or no-shoot that shot will not count for score or penalty, as the case may be. If it cannot be determined which hit(s) struck wholly within hard cover and subsequently struck another cardboard target, a reshoot shall be ordered.

9.1.6.2   If a bullet strikes wholly within hard cover and continues on to hit a plate or strike down a popper; this will be treated as range equipment failure (see Section 4.6). The competitor will be required to reshoot the course of fire, after it has been restored.

9.1.6.3   If a bullet or slug strikes partially within hard cover and continues on to strike the scoring area of a cardboard target the hit on that cardboard target will count for score or penalty, as the case may be.

9.1.6.4   If a bullet or slug strikes partially within hard cover and continues on to strike down a scoring metal target the fallen target will count for score. If a bullet strikes partially within hard cover and continues on to strike down or hit a metal no-shoot, the fallen no-shoot or hit thereon will count for penalty.

9.1.7   Target sticks and barrier supports (see 2.2.3.5 and definition of Barrier Supports in Appendix A3) are neither Hard Cover nor Soft Cover. Shots which have passed wholly or partially through target sticks and or barrier supports, and which hit a cardboard or metal target will count for score or penalty, as the case may be.

9.1.8   Hits from birdshot or buckshot on a scoring or no shoot cardboard target will not count for score unless the course description calls for engaging cardboard targets with buckshot. Then buckshot hits on both scoring targets and no-shoot targets will count.

9.2   Traditional USPSA Hit Factor Scoring

9.2.1   The written stage briefing for each course of fire must specify one of the following 2 scoring methods:

9.2.1.1   **"Comstock"** – Unlimited time stops on the last shot, unlimited number of shots to be fired, stipulated number of hits per target to count for score.

9.2.1.1.1   A competitor's score is calculated by adding the highest value stipulated number of hits per target, minus penalties, divided by the total time (recorded to two decimal places) taken by the competitor to complete the course of fire, to arrive at a hit factor. The overall stage results are factored by awarding the competitor with the highest hit factor the maximum points available for the course of fire, with all other competitors ranked relatively below the stage winner.

9.2.1.2   **"Limited Time Comstock"**

9.2.1.2.1   In order for match flow it may be necessary to limit times per shooter on long range rifle stages. May be used only for Rifle stages that have rifle targets set at least 100 yards away. When the shooter "times out," the stage is scored as shot including any misses and FTSA penalties. The max time is the time recorded.

9.2.1.2.2 Minimum length of "max time" is 180 seconds on a long course and 30 seconds per string on a standards course, maximum of 3 strings.

9.2.1.2.3 "Limited Time Comstock" must be included in the course description along with the time limit.

9.2.2 Stage results must rank competitors within the relevant Division in descending order of individual stage points achieved, calculated to 4 decimal places.

9.2.3 Match results must rank competitors within the relevant Division in descending order of the combined total of individual stage points achieved calculated to 4 decimal places.

9.2.4 Scoring and Penalty Values

9.2.4.1 Scoring hits on authorized targets will be scored in accordance with the values assigned such targets. (See Appendix B1)

9.2.4.2 Each hit visible on the scoring area of a cardboard no shoot will be penalized the equivalent of twice the point value of a maximum scoring hit.

9.2.4.3 For rifle targets, each full or partial diameter hit visible on the frontal surface of a metal no-shoot will be penalized the equivalent of twice the point value of a maximum scoring hit, regardless of whether or not it is designed to fall. (See Rules 4.3.5 and 9.5.3.5.) Shotgun no-shoot metal targets must be shot and fall or overturn to score and then will be penalized the equivalent of twice the point value of a maximum scoring hit.

9.2.4.4 Each miss will be penalized twice the value of the maximum scoring hit available on that target, except in the case of disappearing targets. (See Rule 9.9.2.)

9.2.5 **Optional Enhanced Target Values**

Certain targets may prove to be "not worth shooting" when the standard target values are used (5 points for clays, 5 or 10 points for rifle and shotgun steel). Using an extreme example, a plate at 500 yards may be "not worth shooting" given that the 5 or 10 points gained for a hit would likely cost the average shooter an inordinate amount of time.

9.2.5.1 Frangible flying targets will be scored at 10-point value with an option of 20-point value should the Match Director choose and are to be considered disappeared once they land. On rifle courses, frangible targets will usually score 10 points, but the Match Director may choose 20 points.

9.2.5.2 Steel handgun target values may be doubled (10 points) at distances beyond 50 yards. Use of steel handgun targets beyond 50 yards is discouraged.

9.2.5.3   Steel shotgun shot target values may be increased 10 points (to 15 points or 20 points) at distances beyond 20 yards. Use of steel shotgun shot targets beyond 35 yards is discouraged.

9.2.5.4   Steel shotgun slug target values may be increased 10 points (to 15 points or 20 points) at distances beyond 50 yards. Use of steel shotgun slug targets beyond 100 yards is discouraged.

9.2.5.5   Steel rifle target values may be increased 10 points for each 100 yards of distance

— 0-99 yards value is 5 or 10 points
— 100-199 yards value may be up to 20 points
— 200-299 yards value may be up to 30 points
— 300-399 yards value may be up to 40 points

9.2.5.6   Enhanced target values for steel should comply with the following constraints:

9.2.5.6.1   Enhanced target values are defined at the discretion of the course designer or match director, before the match begins. There is no requirement that steel target values be enhanced; this only provides an option that the course designer may use to make targets "worth shooting."

9.2.5.6.2   Enhanced target values should be used only to ensure competitive equity and to remove any competitive "benefit" which might arise by choosing to ignore a distant target. Enhanced target values should not be used abusively or punitively. (e.g., Assigning high target values to difficult shots resulting in a large number of "zero-scores" on a stage.)

9.2.5.6.3   Enhanced target values should be used sparingly, in order to preserve "balance" in the stage designs. It is recommended that no more than 50% of the points in any stage be derived from "enhanced target values."

9.2.5.7   Enhanced target values apply to steel or thrown/launched frangible targets only. Providing enhanced scoring values for cardboard targets is prohibited.

9.2.5.8   Stage descriptions must clearly identify enhanced-value targets.

9.2.5.8.1   It is NOT required that all steel on a stage have the same value. Steel target values may be mixed on a single stage.

9.2.5.8.2 Except as specified in Rule 10.2.11 and exception 10.2.13, procedural penalties are assessed at twice the value of a single maximum available scoring hit on a cardboard target as stated in Appendix B1. If the maximum available scoring hit on a cardboard target is 5 points, each procedural penalty will be minus 10 points.

9.2.6 The minimum score for a course of fire or string will be zero.

9.2.7 Chronograph and Power Factors

9.2.7.1 One or more official match chronographs are used to assist in the determination of the power factor of every competitor's ammunition. In the absence of official match chronograph(s), the power factor declared by a competitor cannot be challenged. (This section does not apply to Shotgun matches.)

9.2.7.1.1 The power factor rating to enable a competitor's scores to be included in match results is called "Minor." Some Divisions offer a higher power factor rating called "Major," which enables competitors to earn more points for peripheral shots on scoring cardboard targets.

9.2.7.1.2 The power factor floor for Minor rating and the power factor floor for Major rating, if available, and other specific requirements applicable to each Division are stipulated in Appendices D1 to D5.

9.2.7.1.3 The associated values awarded for Minor and Major scoring hits are illustrated in Appendix B1.

9.2.7.1 The method used to determine power factor and the procedures used at the Chronograph Station are stipulated in Appendix C2.

9.3 Time Plus Scoring

9.3.1 Unless otherwise stipulated in the written stage briefing, any cardboard target designated as a "shoot" target must be neutralized by either one (1) "A" hit - OR - two (2) hits anywhere inside the scoring perforations on the target (i.e. minimum 2 "D" hits) to avoid a penalty.

9.3.1.1 Optional scoring - Course description may stipulate that for shotgun one slug hit anywhere in the scoring area will neutralize a cardboard target.

9.3.2 Scoring penalties

9.3.2.1 One C or D hit only = 5 second penalty (Failure to neutralize)

9.3.2.2 No hits on cardboard target but target was engaged = 10 second penalty per target

9.3.2.3 A miss on a frangible, knock down or self-indicating target that was engaged = 10 second penalty per target. See Section 9.5.3 for scoring specifics.

9.3.2.4 A failure to engage any target adds a 5 second penalty to any miss penalties for the target not engaged. An additional procedural penalty is not assessed in this case. (See Rule 10.2.7.)

9.3.2.5 Designated "No Shoot" targets that are hit will incur a 5 second penalty for each hit.

9.3.2.6 Procedural penalties (Section 10.2) are 5 seconds added to the shooters time per procedural. (Exceptions: Rules 9.3.2.4 and 10.2.13.)

9.3.2.7 In the course description, long range rifle targets may be designated as enhanced penalty targets. A miss on an enhanced penalty targets can be increased to a 15 or a 20 second penalty. This is only to be used for targets beyond 100 yards.

9.3.3 In order for match flow it may be necessary to limit times per shooter on long range rifle stages and may be used only for Rifle or Multigun stages that have rifle targets set at least 100 yards away. When the shooter "times out," the stage is scored as shot including any misses and FTSA penalties. The max time is the time recorded. Minimum time limit is 180 seconds. Time limits should be set for match flow and not as a penalty for slower shooters or to create a fixed time stage. If not specified, the maximum time for any stage (including target penalties) is 500 seconds.

9.3.4 Flying clay targets. The course description must stipulate if they are to be scored as bonus targets or as a regular target. Bonuses are scored as time off the shooter's stage time and the amount should reflect the difficulty of the target itself. When scored as a regular target miss penalties are applied. No FTSA penalty will be applied to flying clay targets.

9.3.5 Power Factors do not apply to Time Plus scoring and there is no minimum power factor.

9.3.6 Stage Points - First Place (lowest time) for each stage, in each division, will receive 100 points; Second Place and below will figure points on a percentage basis of the 100 from 1st Place.

9.3.7 Total points accumulated for all stages will determine the match placement by division.

9.3.8 Highest score wins.

9.4 Scoring Ties

9.4.1 If in the opinion of the Match Director a tie in match results must be broken the affected competitors must shoot one or more courses of fire nominated or created by the Match Director until the tie is broken. The result of a tiebreaker will only be used to determine the final placing of the affected competitors and their original match points will remain unchanged. Ties must never be broken by chance.

9.5 Scoring Policy

9.5.1 Unless otherwise specified in the written stage briefing, scoring cardboard targets must be shot with a minimum of one round each. Scoring metal targets must be shot with a minimum of one round each and must fall (or otherwise react in the case of a rifle or shotgun target) to score. Frangible targets (PCC, rifle and shotgun only) must break with a visible piece missing or separated from the original target to be counted for score.

9.5.2 **Cardboard Targets**

9.5.2.1 If the bullet diameter of a hit on a scoring target touches the scoring line between two scoring areas, or the line between the non-scoring border and a scoring area, or if it crosses multiple scoring areas, it will be scored the higher value.

9.5.2.1.1 Additionally, Rule 9.5.2.1 is clarified to apply only to the visible portions of targets. It specifically does not apply to any area of any target which is in direct contact with and overlapped by the scoring area of another target (scoring and/or no-shoots) or by hard cover.

9.5.2.2 If a bullet diameter touches the scoring area of both a scoring target and a no-shoot it will earn the score and incur the penalty.

9.5.2.3 Radial tears will not count for score or penalty.

9.5.2.4 Enlarged holes in cardboard targets which exceed the competitor's bullet diameter will not count for score or penalty unless there is visible evidence within the remnants of the hole (e.g., a grease mark or a "crown," etc.) to eliminate a presumption that the hole was caused by a ricochet or splatter.

9.5.2.5 Hits visible on a scoring cardboard target or no-shoot which are the result of shots fired through the rear of the target or no-shoot will not count for score or penalty, as the case may be.

9.5.2.6 Hits upon scoring or no-shoot cardboard targets must completely pass through the target to be considered a valid hit and count for score or penalty.

9.5.2.7   If a shotgun wad has caused an extra hole in a cardboard target and it cannot be determined which hole has been caused by the actual slug the competitor must reshoot the stage.

9.5.2.8   In a Multigun match any hit(s) upon the scoring surface of a scoring cardboard target which can be determined to have been fired from the incorrect firearm for that target shall not be scored and, unless there are scoring hit(s) from the correct firearm, it will be scored as an unengaged target. In the case of steel or frangible targets any hits by the non-specified firearm which result in that target being unavailable for further engagement, the target shall be scored as an unengaged target.

9.5.3   **Metal Targets**

9.5.3.1   Scoring metal targets for handgun must be shot and fall or overturn to score. Scoring Poppers which fail to fall when hit are subject to the provisions of Section 4.6. (See also Rule 4.3.4.)

9.5.3.2   Self-indicating metal targets must show a hit as designed to score. ROs may call hits.

9.5.3.3   Metal scoring shotgun plates will be scored as a hit if the plate falls from a hit on the plate, base or supporting stand when the plate is shot at.

9.5.3.4   Self-indicating (flash targets) must flash to score.

9.5.3.5   Metal no-shoot targets which are designed to fall when hit but which fail to fall or overturn when struck by a full or partial diameter hit with a handgun, PCC or rifle shall incur the penalty or penalties and are not grounds for a reshoot per range equipment failure. Shotgun no-shoot targets must fall to incur a penalty.

9.5.3.5.1   Metal no-shoot targets must, if hit, be repainted after each competitor ends their attempt at the course of fire failing which subsequent competitors must not be penalized for hits visible on their surface.

9.5.4   **Frangible Targets** – Frangible targets must break with a visible piece missing or separated from the original target to be counted for score. A fixed frangible target that falls from a hit on its holder will be considered a hit.

9.5.5   A competitor who fails to shoot at the face of each scoring target in a course of fire with at least one round will incur one procedural penalty per target for failure to shoot at the target, as well as appropriate penalties for misses. (See Rule 10.2.7.)

9.6   Score Verification and Challenge

9.6.1   After the Range Officer has declared "Range is Clear" the competitor or their delegate will be allowed to accompany the official responsible for scoring to verify the scoring. However, this may not apply to courses of fire consisting only of reactive targets or self-setting targets and/or electronically registering targets.

9.6.2   The Range Official responsible for a course of fire may stipulate that the scoring process will begin while a competitor is actually completing a course of fire. In such cases, the competitor's delegate must be entitled to accompany the official responsible for scoring in order to verify the scoring. Competitors must be advised of this procedure during the squad briefing.

9.6.3   A competitor (or his delegate) who fails to verify a target during the scoring process loses all right of appeal in respect of scoring that target.

9.6.4   Any challenge to a score or penalty must be appealed to the Range Officer by the competitor (or his delegate) prior to the subject target being painted, patched, or reset, failing which such challenges will not be accepted.

9.6.5   In the event that the Range Officer upholds the original score, or penalty and the competitor is dissatisfied he may appeal to the Chief Range Officer and then to the Range Master for a ruling.

9.6.6   The Range Master's ruling will be final. No further appeals are allowed with respect to the scoring decision.

9.6.7   During a scoring challenge the subject target(s) must not be patched, taped or otherwise interfered with until the matter has been settled. The Range Officer may remove a disputed cardboard target from the course of fire for further examination to prevent any delay in the match. Both the competitor and the Range Officer must sign the target and clearly indicate which hit(s) is (are) subject to challenge.

9.6.8   Official USPSA Overlays approved by the Range Master must be used exclusively, as and when required, to verify and/or determine the applicable scoring zone of hits on cardboard targets. (Does not apply to Shotgun targets.)

9.7   Score Sheets

NOTE: For purposes of these rules, the words "score sheet" and "scoring device" are identical and interchangeable. Score sheet can refer to the paper backup provided to competitors as well.

9.7.1   The Range Officer must enter all information on each competitor's score sheet prior to signing it. After the Range Officer has signed the score sheet the competitor must add his own signature in the appropriate place. Electronic score sheet signatures will be acceptable if approved by the USPSA President. Whole numbers should be used to record all scores or penalties. The elapsed time taken by the competitor to complete the course of fire must be recorded to 2 decimal places in the appropriate place.

9.7.2   If corrections to the score sheet are required, these will be clearly entered onto the original and other copies of the competitor's score sheets. Changes and corrections must be logged by the electronic scoring system in use at the match. The competitor and the Range Officer should initial or verbally agree to any corrections. Corrections are defined as modifications to the score sheet before the RO and Competitor sign off on the score sheet.

9.7.3   Should a competitor refuse to sign or initial a score sheet, or scoring device for any reason, the matter must be referred to the Range Master. If the Range Master is satisfied that the course of fire has been conducted and scored correctly the unsigned score sheet will be submitted as normal for inclusion in the match scores. The Range Master may touch "approve" to submit the score if necessary.

9.7.4   A score sheet or electronic scoring device signed by both a competitor and a Range Officer is conclusive evidence that the course of fire has been completed, and that the time, scores and penalties recorded on the score sheet are accurate and uncontested. The signed score sheet is deemed to be a definitive document. It may only be changed to add penalties under Rule 8.6.2, or to correct arithmetical errors, or by mutual consent of the competitor and the originating Range Officer, or due to an arbitration decision. Changes are defined as modifications to the score sheet after both parties have signed off on the score sheet. Touching "review" is deemed to be equivalent to the RO signing the device. Touching "approve" is deemed to be equivalent to the competitor signing the device and accepting the score.

9.7.5   If a score sheet or scoring device is found to have insufficient or excess entries, or if the time has not been recorded on the score sheet or device, the competitor will be required to reshoot the course of fire.

9.7.6   In the event that a reshoot is not possible or permissible for any reason the following actions will prevail:

   9.7.6.1   If the time is missing the competitor will receive a zero score for the course of fire.

   9.7.6.2   If insufficient hits or misses have been recorded on the score sheet, the hits and misses which have been recorded will be deemed complete and conclusive. Any missing scores should be recorded in the scoring tally as a no-penalty-miss which does not add or remove points from the competitors score.

   9.7.6.3   If excessive hits or misses have been recorded on the score sheet the highest value scoring hits recorded will be used.

   9.7.6.4   Procedural penalties recorded on the score sheet will be deemed complete and conclusive except where Rule 8.6.2 applies.

   9.7.6.5   If the identity of the competitor is missing from a score sheet it must be referred to the Range Master who must take whatever action he deems necessary to rectify the situation.

9.7.7   In the event that an original score sheet is lost or otherwise unavailable the competitor's duplicate copy, or any other written or electronic record acceptable to the Range Master will be used. If the competitor's copy or any other written or electronic record is unavailable or is deemed by the Range Master to be insufficiently legible, the competitor will be required to reshoot the course of fire. If the Range Master deems that a reshoot is not possible for any reason the competitor will incur a zero score for the affected course of fire.

9.8   Scoring Responsibility

9.8.1   Each competitor is responsible to maintain an accurate record of their scores to verify the results posted by the Stats Officer.

9.8.2   After all competitors have completed a match; the provisional stage results should be published and posted in a conspicuous place, either at the shooting range or electronically, by the Stats Officer for the purpose of verification by competitors.

9.8.3   If a competitor detects an error in the provisional results at the end of the match, they must file an appeal with the Stats Officer not later than 1 hour after the results are posted. At level I and level II matches only, providing scores have been made available to all competitors on a regular basis throughout the match (e.g., electronic posting), this one-hour review period may be waived by a majority vote of the competitors present. At Level III matches only, the Match Director may set the review period time to less than 1 hour, providing scores have been made available to all competitors on a regular basis throughout the match (e.g. electronic posting). The reduced time period must be published in advance in match literature or by way of a notice via electronic communications or posted in a conspicuous place at the shooting range. If the appeal is not filed within the time limit, the posted scores will stand, and the appeal will be dismissed.

9.8.4   Competitors who are scheduled (or otherwise authorized by a Match Director) to complete all courses of fire in a match in a period of time less than the full duration of the match (e.g., 1-day format in a 3-day match etc.), are required to check their provisional match results in accordance with the special procedures and time limits specified by the Match Director (e.g., via a website) failing which scoring appeals will not be accepted. The relevant procedure must be published in advance in match literature and/or by way of a notice posted in a conspicuous place at the shooting range prior to commencement of the match.

9.9 Scoring of Activated Targets

9.9.1   Non-disappearing and Visible Targets: Activated scoring targets which present a legal portion of the A-zone, either prior to activation or when they stop (gravity operated), or which continuously appear and disappear (motorized), will always incur failure to shoot at and miss penalties. At least 25% of the lower A-zone or all of the upper A-zone must be visible to be legal. If the target is legally visible before being activated, it may be shot before being activated and activation is not required (9.9.3 does not apply).

9.9.2   Disappearing and Appearing targets: Activated scoring targets which do not comply with the above criteria are considered disappearing targets and will not incur failure to shoot at or miss penalties, unless they are not activated (Rule 9.9.3 applies). In Time Plus scoring, disappearing targets may be designated as bonus targets. Bonuses are scored as time off the shooter's stage time and the amount should reflect the difficulty of the target itself.

9.9.3   Activated appearing scoring targets will always incur failure to shoot at and miss penalties if a competitor does not activate the target movement either before or with the last shot fired in a course of fire. This includes no-shoot targets that must be activated to expose scoring targets. This does not apply to legally presented targets that are available to be shot prior to activation (9.9.1). Penalties are based on number of shots required for the activated scoring target or the scoring target(s) behind the no-shoot.

9.9.4   Level I matches only - If the written stage briefing prohibits the engagement of certain targets prior to activation the competitor will incur one procedural penalty per shot fired at such targets prior to initiating the activating mechanism up to the maximum number of available hits. (See Rule 2.1.8.4.1.)

9.10 Official Time

9.10.1   Only the timing device operated by a Range Officer must be used to record the official elapsed time of a competitor's attempt at a course of fire. If a timing device is faulty a competitor whose attempt cannot be credited with an accurate time will be required to reshoot the stage.

9.10.2   If in the opinion of an Arbitration Committee, the time credited to a competitor for a course of fire is deemed to be unrealistic the competitor will be required to reshoot the course of fire. (See Rule 9.7.4.)

9.10.3   A competitor who reacts to a start signal but, for any reason, does not fire a shot or continue the attempt at the course of fire and fails to have an official time recorded on the timing device operated by the Range Officer will be given a zero score for that course of fire. This constitutes a Did Not Fire, or DNF for the stage.

9.11 Scoring Programs

9.11.1   The scoring program approved by USPSA is PractiScore. No other scoring program must be used for any USPSA sanctioned match without the prior written approval of the President of USPSA. Handheld electronic tablets/devices may be used for the collection and dissemination of scoring data.

9.11.2   When electronic scoring is used, once stage scoring is completed, every competitor shall be provided the opportunity to read and approve the scoring device to review their stage time and score entries. At Level II or higher matches, range officers shall also create a hard copy record that includes the hit and penalty totals, time, hit factor, time of day, competitor initials and range officer initials for each stage. This procedure may only be waived with permission from the USPSA President. If there is a discrepancy between the hard copy record and PractiScore, and the hit factors are identical, then the PractiScore entry will be definitive.

CHAPTER 10 – Penalties

10.1 Procedural Penalties – General Regulations

10.1.1 Procedural penalties are imposed when a competitor fails to comply with procedures specified in a written stage briefing. The Range Officer imposing the procedural penalties must clearly record the number of penalties and the reason why they were imposed on the competitor's score sheet.

10.1.2 A competitor disputing the application or number of procedural penalties may appeal to the Chief Range Officer and then to the Range Master. A competitor who continues to be aggrieved may then lodge an appeal for arbitration.

10.1.3 Procedural penalties cannot be nullified by further competitor action. For example, a competitor who fires a shot at a target while faulting a line will still incur the applicable penalties even though he subsequently shoots at the same target while not faulting the line.

10.2 Procedural Penalties – Specific Examples

10.2.1 If a competitor fires shots while touching the ground or any object completely outside the fault lines, they will be assessed one procedural penalty per occurrence. If any part of an object is inside the fault lines, then that entire object may be used for support without penalty. Support structures outside the shooting area such as, but not limited to wall feet, legs, braces, etc., may never be used for support, and any object completely outside the fault lines may not be used for support, even if it touches an object that is inside the fault lines. Course designers may designate certain parts of structures, such as raised platforms, as part of the shooting area, while excluding their support structure or steps, but must mark those areas with legal fault lines. Raised planks or timbers may be designated as shooting areas as long as they satisfy the requirements listed in 2.2.1.2. Using or touching objects outside the shooting area to steady or support a long gun is permissible as long as the competitor is not otherwise faulting as described above. No penalty is assessed if a competitor does not fire any shots while faulting, providing doing so does not violate 2.2.1.5 or 3.2.6.

    10.2.1.1 However, if the competitor has gained a significant advantage on any target(s) while faulting, the competitor may instead be assessed one procedural penalty for each shot fired at the subject target(s) while faulting. No penalty is assessed if a competitor does not fire any shots while faulting, providing doing so does not violate 2.2.1.5 or 3.2.6.

    10.2.1.2 Shots fired after completely (both feet out and touching the ground) leaving a shooting area, will be penalized one penalty per shot until the competitor establishes a presence in a new shooting area with at least one foot on the ground inside the shooting area.

10.2.1.3　If a competitor starts and fires shots while completely outside a shooting area, foot fault penalties will apply as above, as stated in 10.2.1 and/or 10.2.1.1.

10.2.2　A competitor who fails to comply with a procedure specified in the written stage briefing will incur one procedural penalty for each occurrence. However, if a competitor has gained a significant advantage during non-compliance, the competitor may be assessed one procedural penalty for each shot fired, instead of a single penalty (e.g., firing multiple shots contrary to the required position or stance).

10.2.3　Where multiple penalties are assessed in the above cases, they must not exceed the maximum number of scoring hits that can be attained by the competitor. For example, a competitor who gains an advantage while faulting a Fault Line where only four metal targets are visible will receive one procedural penalty for each shot fired while faulting, up to a maximum of four procedural penalties, regardless of number of shots fired.

10.2.4　A competitor who fails to comply with a mandatory reload will incur one procedural penalty for each shot fired after the point where the reload was required until a reload is performed.

10.2.5　In a Cooper Tunnel a competitor who disturbs one or more pieces of the overhead material will receive one procedural penalty for each piece of overhead material which falls during the course of fire. Overhead material which falls as a result of the competitor bumping or striking the uprights, or as a result of muzzle gases, recoil, or an ejected case will not be penalized.

10.2.6　A competitor who is creeping (e.g., moving hands towards the firearm, a reloading device or ammunition) or physically moving to a more advantageous shooting position or posture at the start signal, will incur one procedural penalty.

10.2.6.1　Exception: any movement required or specified in the stage briefing (e.g., self-start) will not be penalized.

10.2.7　A competitor who fails to shoot at any scoring target with at least one round will incur one procedural penalty per target, plus the applicable number of misses, except where the provisions of Rules 9.2.4.4 or 9.9.2 apply.

10.2.8　If a course of fire stipulates shooting strong or weak hand only a competitor will not be penalized for using the other hand (i.e., the other arm from the shoulder to the hand) to disengage an external safety, to reload or to correct a malfunction. However, the competitor will be issued one procedural penalty per shot fired while:

10.2.8.1　Touching the handgun with the other hand, or using the wrong hand, while firing shots;

10.2.8.2 Using the other hand to support the handgun, wrist or shooting arm while firing shots.

10.2.8.3 Using the other hand on a barricade or another prop to increase stability while firing shots.

10.2.8.4 If a course of fire stipulates the use of the weak side only the competitor will be issued procedural penalties for using the strong side. This will be assessed as 1 procedural penalty per shot fired.

10.2.9 A competitor who leaves a shooting location may return and shoot again.

10.2.10 A competitor who engages a target while transitioning to another firearm will receive a procedural penalty per shot fired while handling both firearms. (See Rule 8.4.2.2.)

10.2.11 Special penalty: A competitor unable to fully execute any part of a course of fire due to incapacity or injury may, prior to making his attempt at the course of fire, request that the Range Master apply a penalty in lieu of the stated course requirement. The penalty should be only used to negate any advantage gained by the competitor not fulfilling the course requirement. The Range Master may waive any or all procedural penalties in respect of a competitor who has a significant physical disability prior to the competitor making his attempt at the course of fire if no advantage is gained.

10.2.11.1 Exception – In a weak hand/strong hand stage a competitor who has physical use of only one hand may use the same hand for both weak and strong without penalty.

10.2.12 Should a competitor with a full auto capable firearm shoot at a target or targets with burst or fully automatic fire (where more than one shot is discharged with one manipulation of the trigger) he will be scored zero for that stage and a warning issued. In the event of another infraction he will be disqualified from the match. Use of a trigger mechanism which allows one shot to be fired upon pulling the trigger and one to be fired upon releasing the trigger will incur a match disqualification.

10.2.13 Abandoning a loaded firearm in the retention device with safety off will result in a procedural penalty of 30 seconds in time plus scoring or 3 procedurals in traditional Comstock scoring.

10.2.13.1 If the safety is partially engaged and firearm is in battery the RO will clear downrange and remove any magazine. Then, pointing the firearm downrange, he will attempt to fire it. If it does not fire no penalty will apply. If it fires the penalty will apply.

10.2.13.2 A jammed firearm is still considered loaded and must have the safety fully on when abandoned to avoid a penalty.

10.3 Match Disqualification – General Regulations

10.3.1   A competitor or staff member who commits a safety infraction or any other prohibited activity during a USPSA match will be disqualified from that match. When the safety infraction or prohibited activity is caused by a medical condition the competitor or staff member will be prohibited from attempting any remaining courses of fire and duties in that match regardless of the schedule or physical layout of the match. The Director of NROI shall be notified immediately. (A Multigun match is considered a single match.)

10.3.2   When a match disqualification is issued the Range Officer must record the reasons for the disqualification, and the time and date of the incident on the competitor's score sheet and the Range Master must be notified as soon as possible.

10.3.3   Scores for a competitor who has received a match disqualification must not be deleted from match results and match results must not be declared final by the Match Director until the time limit prescribed in Rule 11.3.1 has passed, provided no appeal to arbitration on any matter has been submitted to the Range Master (or his delegate).

10.3.4   If an appeal to arbitration is submitted within the time limit prescribed in Rule 11.3.1, the provisions of Rule 11.3.2 will prevail.

10.3.5   Scores for a competitor who has completed a "pre-match" or main match without a match disqualification will not be affected by a match disqualification received later while that competitor is participating in a Shoot-Off or other side match.

10.3.6   Commission of a forbidden action as defined in rule 3.2.6.1 shall result in match disqualification.

10.3.7   Climbing or standing on an object that is not specifically designed and intended for that purpose and identified in the written stage briefing as permitted to be used for that purpose shall result in match disqualification. Shooting boxes and fault lines are exempt from this rule.

10.4 Match Disqualification – Accidental Discharge

A competitor who causes an accidental discharge must be stopped by a Range Officer as soon as possible. An accidental discharge is defined as follows:

10.4.1   A shot which travels over a backstop, a berm or in any other direction specified in the written stage briefing by the match organizers as being unsafe. Note that a competitor who legitimately fires a shot at a target which then travels in an unsafe direction will not be disqualified. (The provisions of Section 2.3 may apply).

     10.4.1.1   Exception- engaging flying targets with birdshot. Rule 10.5.2 still applies.

10.4.2 A shot which strikes the ground within 10 feet of the competitor except when shooting at a cardboard or frangible target closer than 10 feet to the competitor.

    10.4.2.1 Exception — A bullet which strikes the ground within 10 feet of the competitor due to a "squib."

    10.4.2.2 In the case of a shot striking a prop where the bullet is deflected or does not continue to strike the ground, if the Range Official determines that the bullet would have struck the ground within 10 feet of the competitor had it not been deflected or stopped by the prop, the provisions of Rule 10.4.2 shall apply.

10.4.3 A shot which occurs while loading, preloading, reloading or unloading a firearm. This includes any shot fired during the procedures outlined in Rules 8.3.7.

    10.4.3.1 Exception – a detonation which occurs while unloading a firearm is not considered a shot or discharge subject to a match disqualification. However, Rule 5.1.7 may apply.

10.4.4 A shot which occurs during remedial action in the case of a malfunction.

    10.4.4.1 Exception – a detonation which occurs while unloading a firearm is not considered a shot or discharge subject to a match disqualification. However, Rule 5.1.7 may apply.

10.4.5 A shot which occurs while transferring a firearm between hands or shoulders.

10.4.6 A shot which occurs during movement except while actually shooting at targets.

10.4.7 A shot which occurs while abandoning or retrieving a staged firearm, when the competitor is not engaging targets, and the shot does not strike a target.

10.5 Match Disqualification – Unsafe Gun Handling

Examples of unsafe gun handling include, but are not limited to:

10.5.1 Handling a firearm at any time except when in a designated safety area (or in the case of long guns, elsewhere deemed safe by a Range Officer), or when under the supervision of and in response to a direct command issued by a Range Officer. This includes deliberately removing a flag from a long gun except under the conditions listed here. This does not apply to the carrying of PCCs, rifles, or shotguns where Rule 5.2.2 will apply.

10.5.2 If at any time during the course of fire a competitor allows the muzzle of his firearm to point rearwards, that is further than 90 degrees from the median intercept of the backstop, or in the case of no backstop allows the muzzle to point uprange, whether the firearm is loaded or not. (Limited exceptions:

Rules <u>10.5.5</u> and <u>8.2.7</u>.) An abandoned firearm found to be pointed in an unsafe direction will be considered a violation. When abandoned in a vertically set barrel any muzzle down orientation is considered a safe direction.

10.5.3 If at any time during the course of fire, or while loading, preloading, reloading or unloading a competitor drops his firearm, or causes it to fall, loaded or not.

    10.5.3.1 A competitor who for any reason during a course of fire safely and intentionally places the firearm on the ground or other stable object will not be disqualified provided the competitor maintains constant physical contact with the firearm until it is placed firmly and in a safe direction, securely on the ground or another stable object, and remains within 1 yard of the firearm at all times. Firing a second firearm while a firearm has been placed in this manner will result in a DQ.

    10.5.3.2 Abandoning a loaded firearm outside of the retention device will result in a Match DQ. Note: If the shooter remains within 1 yard of the firearm as specified in Rule <u>10.5.3.1</u> the firearm is not considered abandoned.

10.5.4 Allowing the muzzle to point at any part of any person's body during a course of fire (i.e., sweeping). This includes anyone passing in front of the muzzle of an abandoned firearm whether they are the current shooter or not. Non-shooters (i.e., spectators or other people) may be subject to <u>10.6.2</u> for violation. If the RO is swept, the Range Master must be called to determine if it was RO interference or a DQ.

    10.5.4.1 Exception – A match disqualification is not applicable for sweeping of the lower extremities (below the belt) while drawing or re-holstering of the handgun provided that the competitor's fingers are clearly outside of the trigger guard. This exception is only for holstered handguns.

    10.5.4.2 Failing to point the muzzle of any firearm at a side berm or back stop during casing or uncasing. The berm/backstop is not required while removing/returning a properly flagged long gun from/to a vehicle providing all other safety rules are followed.

    10.5.4.3 Sweeping any person with the muzzle of any firearm, whether loaded or not, even if a chamber flag is inserted, at any time during the match.

10.5.5 While facing downrange, allowing the muzzle of a loaded handgun to point uprange beyond a radius of 3 feet from a competitor's feet while drawing or re-holstering.

10.5.6	Having more than one handgun, one rifle, one shotgun, and one pistol caliber carbine at any point in time during a course of fire. (This does not apply to match supplied prop guns or a match requiring a fifth firearm such as a bolt rifle.)
10.5.7	Failure to keep the finger outside the trigger guard while clearing a malfunction.
10.5.8	Failure to keep the finger outside the trigger guard during loading, preloading, reloading, or unloading. (Exceptions: While complying with the "Make Ready" command to lower the hammer of a gun without a decocking lever.)
10.5.9	Failure to keep the finger outside the trigger guard during movement in accordance with Section 8.5.
10.5.10	Holstering a loaded handgun in any of the following conditions:
10.5.10.1	A single action self-loading handgun with the safety not applied.
10.5.10.2	A double action or selective action handgun with the hammer cocked and the safety not applied.
10.5.10.3	A revolver with the hammer cocked.
10.5.10.4	If the primary safety on the firearm cannot be engaged due to the design of the firearm, and the hammer/trigger cannot be actuated in the condition the gun is in, the safety does not have to be applied. For example, a loaded handgun, per our definition, is one with a loaded magazine inserted into the magazine well. In a 1911 or similar design pistol, if the slide is not racked, and the hammer is not back, the safety cannot be applied. Although this gun is by definition loaded, it is considered to be in a safe condition if the hammer is down and the safety cannot physically be applied. In the event of doubt the Range Master is the final authority on this matter.

All these conditions apply the entire time the handgun is in the holster. See 8.1.2.4

10.5.11	Handling live or dummy ammunition (including practice or training rounds, snap caps and empty cases), loaded magazines or loaded speed loading devices in a Safety Area. The word "handling" does not preclude competitors from entering a Safety Area with ammunition in magazines or speed loading devices on their belt, in their pockets or in their range bag provided the competitor does not physically remove the loaded magazines or loaded speed loading devices from their retaining or storage device while within the Safety Area.
10.5.12	Having a loaded firearm other than when specifically ordered to by the

Range Officer. See the Glossary for the definition of a loaded firearm.

10.5.13   Retrieving a dropped firearm. A dropped firearm must always be retrieved by a Range Officer who will ensure it is unloaded and properly secured in the competitor's holster or a suitable container. The Range Officer may, at his discretion, secure the gun himself or return it to the competitor who will secure it under supervision of the Range Officer.

Dropping an unloaded firearm or causing it to fall outside of a course of fire is not an infraction; however, a competitor who retrieves a dropped handgun will receive a match disqualification.

10.5.13.1 If a competitor's gun is partially dislodged from his holster while outside a COF, and the competitor "traps" the gun in the holster (trigger not exposed) he may do so without penalty. The competitor should immediately proceed to a safe area and address any necessary equipment issues.

10.5.13.2 If the competitor's gun has left the holster (trigger exposed) the gun must be treated as dropped. Even if the competitor is able to "trap" the gun before it falls to the ground he must safely and securely lower the gun to the ground and call for a RO to safely retrieve it.

10.5.14   Using metal piercing, steel core or jacketed, steel shot, or any round or shot containing tungsten, any incendiary and/or tracer ammunition (see Rule 5.5.5), and/or using any ammunition which has been deemed unsafe by a Range Official at any time during the match or on a course of fire regardless of target types engaged. (See Rules 5.5.7 and 5.5.8.)

10.5.14.1 Ammunition declared unsafe by a Range Official due to multiple squibs, shall not subject the competitor to disqualification unless the competitor fails to remove that ammunition from the match as directed.

10.5.15   Drawing a handgun while facing uprange or while prone.

10.5.16   Firing a shot at a metal target from a distance of less than 23 feet with a handgun, 147 feet with a rifle, 16 feet with a shotgun when using birdshot or buckshot ammunition, or 147 feet when using slug ammunition. The distance is measured from the face of the target to the nearest part of the competitor's body in contact with the ground. (See Rule 2.1.3.)

10.5.17   Re-slinging any firearm during a Course of Fire. (Once unslung and a round is chambered for use a firearm must not be re-slung. See 8.5.2.)

10.5.18   Firearms capable of fully automatic or burst fire, (one trigger pull results in firing more than one shot, and stocks or other devices that are capable of bump fire are not prohibited, providing they are not used in full auto, burst, or bump fire mode. Use of binary triggers (one pull and release of the trigger results in firing more than one shot), is prohibited. Use of such devices in full auto, burst, binary or bump fire mode, will result in a procedural penalty for the first occurrence, and a disqualification for any subsequent infractions. Bump firing without mechanical aid is not penalized, provided there are no other equipment or safety infractions, the firearm is not doubling, and it can be safely fired in semi-auto mode.

10.5.19 Attempting to clear a squib during a course of fire is considered unsafe gun handling and the competitor is subject to disqualification.

10.5.20 Failing to point the muzzle of a long gun at a side berm or back stop during casing/uncasing or removing/replacing on a conveyance or sweeping any person with the muzzle of a long gun, whether loaded or not, even if a chamber flag is inserted. Side berms/backstops may be used for casing and uncasing or removing from/placing on conveyances only. All other gun handling with the long gun, e.g., cleaning, dry-fire, repairs, etc., must be accomplished in a safety area or under the direct supervision of a Range Officer. Checking if dot is on/off, removing dot cover, and turning dot on/off may be done at casing/uncasing area provided the long gun is flagged and the muzzle remains in a safe direction. The berm/backstop is not required while removing/returning a properly flagged long gun from/to a vehicle providing all other safety rules are followed.

10.6 Match Disqualification – Unsportsmanlike Conduct

10.6.1 Competitors will be disqualified from a match for conduct which a Range Officer deems to be unsportsmanlike. Examples of unsportsmanlike conduct include, but are not limited to cheating, dishonesty, failing to comply with the reasonable directions of a Match Official, or any behavior likely to bring the sport into disrepute. The Range Master must be notified as soon as possible.

10.6.2 Competitors and other persons may be expelled from the range for conduct which a Range Officer deems to be unacceptable. Examples of unacceptable conduct include but are not limited to failing to comply with the reasonable directions of a Match Official, interference with the operation of a course of fire and/or a competitor's attempt thereof, and any other behavior likely to bring the sport into disrepute.

10.6.3 A competitor who is deemed by a Range Officer to have intentionally removed or caused the loss of eye or ear protection in order to gain a competitive advantage will be disqualified.

10.7 Match Disqualification – Prohibited Substances

10.7.1 All persons are required to be in complete control both mentally and physically during USPSA matches.

10.7.2 USPSA considers the abuse of alcoholic products, prescription, nonprescription and non-essential drugs and the use of illegal or performance enhancing drugs, irrespective of how they are taken or administered to be an extremely serious offense.

10.7.3   Except when used for medicinal purposes competitors and officials at matches must not be affected by drugs (including alcohol) of any sort during matches. Any person who in the opinion of the Range Master is visibly under the influence of any of the items described herein will be disqualified from the match and may be required to leave the range.

10.7.4   USPSA reserves the right to prohibit any general or specific substances and to introduce tests for the presence of these substances at any time.

CHAPTER 11 – Arbitration & Interpretation of Rules

11.1 General Principles

11.1.1   Administration – Occasional disputes are inevitable in any competitive activity governed by rules. It is recognized that at the more significant match levels the outcome is much more important to the individual competitor. However, effective match administration and planning will prevent most if not all disputes.

11.1.2   Access – Appeals may be submitted to arbitration in accordance with the following rules for any matter except where specifically denied by another rule. Appeals arising from a disqualification for a safety infraction will only be accepted to determine whether exceptional circumstances warrant reconsideration of the match disqualification. However, the commission of the infraction as described by the Range Official is not subject to challenge or appeal. Challenges to the construction or layout of the course, safety, or shooting conditions may not be submitted after the competitor attempts the course of fire. Should a course of fire be changed after the competitor completes the stage, he is entitled to the process under appeals providing that no DQ has occurred.

11.1.3   Appeals – the Range officer makes decisions initially. If the appellant disagrees with a decision, the Chief Range Officer for the stage or area in question should be asked to rule. If a disagreement still exists, the Range Master must be asked to rule. At no time in the appeals process will audio, video, or photographic evidence be used or considered.

11.1.4   Appeal to Committee – Should the appellant continue to disagree with the decision he may appeal to the Arbitration Committee by submitting a first party appeal.

11.1.5   Retain Evidence – An appellant is required to inform the Range Master of his wish to present his appeal to the Arbitration Committee and may request that the officials retain any and all relevant documentary or other evidence pending the hearing. Photos, audio and/or video recordings will not be accepted as evidence.

11.1.6   Preparing the Appeal – The appellant is responsible for the preparation and delivery of the written submission, together with the appropriate fee. The submission must include relevant rule(s) to support the appeal. Both the submission and the fee must be submitted to the Range Master within the specified period of time. If not properly prepared, the Range Master will return the appeal to the competitor who will prepare it correctly and return it to the Range Master within the specified period of time.

11.1.7   Match Official's Duty – Any Match Official in receipt of a request for arbitration must without delay inform the Range Master and must note the identities of all witnesses and officials involved and pass this information on to the Range Master.

11.1.8　Match Director's Duty – Upon receiving the appeal from the Range Master the Match Director must convene the Arbitration Committee in a place of privacy as soon as possible.

11.1.9　Arbitration Committee's Duty – The Arbitration Committee is bound to observe and apply the current USPSA Rules and to deliver a decision consistent with those rules. Where rules require interpretation or where an incident is not specifically covered by the rules the Arbitration Committee will use their best judgment consistent with the intent of the rules. The Committee must confer with the Match Director before changing or removing a course of fire from the match.

11.2　Composition of Committee

11.2.1　Arbitration Committee – At Level III/Nationals matches the composition of the Arbitration Committee will be subject to the following rules:

11.2.1.1　The Match Director shall appoint a certified Range Official to serve as Chairman of the committee with one vote.

11.2.1.2　The Match Director shall appoint two arbitrators with one vote each.

11.2.1.3　Committee members must be competitors in the match and should be certified Range Officials. Match officials are excluded, with the exception of a staff match.

11.2.1.4　Under no circumstances may the Chairman or any member of an Arbitration Committee be a party to or have a conflict of interest in, the original decision or subsequent appeals which led to the arbitration.

11.2.2　Arbitration Committee – For Level I and Level II matches the Match Director shall appoint an Arbitration Committee of three experienced shooters who are not parties to the appeal and who do not have a direct conflict of interest in the outcome of the case. The arbitrators should be certified Range Officials if possible. All committee members will vote. The senior Range Official, or the senior shooter if there are no Range Officials, will be the chairman.

11.3　Time Limits and Sequences

11.3.1　Time Limit for Arbitration Request – Written requests for arbitration must be submitted to the Range Master within one hour of the disputed incident or occurrence. Failure to present the required documentation within the time specified will render the request invalid and no further action will be taken.

11.3.2　Decision Time Limit – The Committee must reach a decision within 24 hours of the request for arbitration or before the results have been declared final by the Match Director, whichever comes first. If the Committee fails to render a decision within the prescribed period both a first- and third-party appellant (see Section 11.7) will automatically succeed in their appeal and the fee will be returned.

11.4 Fees

11.4.1 Amount – As set by the Match Organizers, the appeal fee to enable an appellant to appeal to arbitration will be US $100 (cash only) or the equivalent of the maximum individual match entry fee (whichever is lower). An appeal brought by the Range Master in respect of a match issue will not incur a fee.

11.4.2 Disbursement and Disposition – If the Committee's decision is to uphold the appeal, the fee paid will be returned to the appellant. If the Committee's decision is to deny the appeal, the appeal fee will be retained by the match. In all cases the arbitration and decision will be forwarded to NROI. All arbitrations will be posted on the USPSA web site.

11.5 Rules of Procedure

11.5.1 Committee's Duty and Procedure – The Committee will study the written submission and retain on behalf of the organizers the monies paid by the appellant until a decision has been reached.

11.5.2 Submissions – The Committee may require the appellant to personally give further details of the submission and may question him on any point relevant to the appeal.

11.5.3 Hearing – The appellant may be asked to withdraw while the Committee hears further evidence.

11.5.4 Witnesses – The Committee may hear Match Officials as well as any other witnesses involved in the appeal. The Committee will examine all evidence submitted.

11.5.5 Questions – The Committee may question witnesses and officials on any point relevant to the appeal.

11.5.6 Opinions – Committee members will refrain from expressing any opinion or verdict while an appeal is in progress.

11.5.7 Inspect Area – The Committee may inspect any range or areas related to the appeal and require any person or official they regard as useful to the process to accompany them.

11.5.8 Undue Influence – Any person attempting to influence the members of the Committee in any way other than evidence may be subject to disciplinary action at the discretion of the Arbitration Committee.

11.5.9 Deliberation – When the Committee is satisfied that they are in possession of all information and evidence relevant to the appeal they will deliberate privately and will reach their decision by majority vote.

11.6 Verdict and Subsequent Action

11.6.1 Committee Decision – All committee decisions must cite the rule(s) on which their decision is based. Committee decisions will be reviewed by the Match Director and Range Master and may be returned to the committee, if necessary, with an explanation of why the decision does not comply with the rules. If the Range Master returns a decision to the Committee, the Committee's next decision must be based on the rules and must be accepted. When a final decision is reached by the Committee, the Match Director will summon the appellant and the official(s) to present its judgment.

11.6.2 Implement Decision – It will be the responsibility of the Range Master to implement the Committee's decision. The Range Master will advise the appropriate match personnel who will post the decision in a place available to all competitors. The decision is not retroactive and will not affect any incidents prior to the decision.

11.6.3 Decision is Final – The decision of the Committee is final and may not be appealed unless, in the opinion of the Range Master, new evidence received after the decision warrants reconsideration.

11.6.4 Minutes – Decisions of the Arbitration Committee will be recorded and will provide precedent for any similar and subsequent incident during that match.

11.7 Third Party Appeals

11.7.1 Appeals may also be submitted by other persons on a "third party appeal" basis. In such cases all provisions of this Chapter will otherwise remain in force.

11.8 Interpretation of Rules

11.8.1 Interpretation of these rules and regulations is the responsibility of the USPSA Director of NROI.

11.8.2 Persons seeking clarification of any rule are required to submit their questions in writing, either by fax, letter or email to NROI headquarters.

11.8.3 All official USPSA interpretations of the rule book published on the USPSA website (www.uspsa.org) will be deemed to be precedents and will be applied to all USPSA matches commencing on or after 7 days from the date of publication. All such interpretations are subject to ratification or modification at a regular or special meeting of the USPSA Board of Directors.

CHAPTER 12 – Miscellaneous Matters

12.1 Appendices

All Appendices included herein are an integral part of these rules.

12.2 Language

English is the official language of the USPSA Rules. Should there be discrepancies between the English language version of these rules and versions presented in other languages the English language version will prevail.

12.3 Disclaimers

Competitors and all other persons in attendance at an USPSA match are wholly, solely and personally responsible to ensure that all and any equipment which they bring to the match is fully in compliance with all laws applicable to the geographical or political area where the match is being held. Neither USPSA nor any USPSA Officers, nor any organization affiliated to USPSA, nor any officers of any organization affiliated to USPSA accepts any responsibility whatsoever in this regard, nor in respect of any loss, damage, accident, injury or death suffered by any person or entity as a result of the lawful or unlawful use of any such equipment.

12.4 Gender

References made herein to the male gender (i.e., "he," "his," or "him") are deemed to include the female gender (i.e., "she" or "her.")

12.5 Measurements

Throughout these rules, with minor exceptions, measurements are expressed in inches, feet or yards. Measurements expressed in mm or cm in brackets are only provided as a guide, except with regard to the dimensions noted for Official Licensed USPSA targets.

APPENDIX A1 — USPSA Match Levels

Level I — Club matches conducted on a regularly scheduled basis throughout the year.

Level II — Sectional and State matches conducted on an annual basis.

Level III — Annual championship matches conducted by USPSA Areas (1 through 8).

Nationals — Annual championship matches conducted by USPSA.

Note: Major matches conducted on an irregular or annual basis and which do not represent a specific Section, State, or Area Championship shall request either Level II or Level III Sanctioning.

Key: N/A = Not Applicable, R = Recommended, M = Mandatory

	Match Level	I	II	III	Nationals
1.	Must follow latest edition USPSA rules	M	M	M	M
2.	Competitors must be USPSA members (Section 6.4)	R	M	M	M
3.	Match Director	M	M	M	M
4.	Range Master (certified or appointed)	M	M	M	M
5.	Certified Range Master	N/A	R*	M	M
6.	Range Master approved by AD	N/A	R**	M	N/A
7.	Range Master approved by NROI	N/A	R**	M	M
8.	Certified Chief Range Officer(s)	R	R	M	M
9.	Minimum one Certified NROI official per stage	R	M	M	M
10.	COF approval by NROI	R	M	M	M
11.	COF submitted to Area Director	N/A	M	M	N/A
12.	NROI Sanctioning	N/A	M	M	M
13.	Chronograph (hit factor scoring only)	R	R	M	M
14.	1-month advance registration with NROI	N/A	M	N/A	N/A
15.	2-month advance registration with NROI	N/A	N/A	M	N/A
16.	Inclusion in USPSA Match Calendar	N/A	M	M	M
17.	Post-match reports to USPSA	N/A	M	M	N/A
18.	Recommended minimum rounds	28	75	150	150
19.	Recommended minimum stages	2	5	8	8
20.	Recommended minimum competitors	10	50	120	120

* **Note: If Range Master is not certified, NROI approval required.**

** **Note: If Range Master is not certified, NROI and Area Director approval required.**

APPENDIX A2 – USPSA Recognition

Prior to the commencement of a match, the organizers must specify which Division(s) will be recognized.

Unless otherwise specified, USPSA sanctioned matches will recognize Divisions and Categories based on the number of registered competitors who actually compete in the match, based on the following criteria:

1. Divisions

Level I/Level II/Level III	A minimum of 5 competitors per Division (recommended)
Nationals	A minimum of 10 competitors per Division (mandatory)

2. Categories

Division status must be achieved before Categories are recognized.

All level matches	A minimum of 5 competitors per Division Category (see approved list below)

3. Individual Categories:

Categories approved for individual recognition are as follows:

Lady	Gender as listed on a government issued ID.
Junior	Competitors who are under the age of 18 on the first day of the match.
Senior	Competitors who are 55-64 years of age on the first day of the match.
Super Senior	Competitors who are 65-69 years of age on the first day of the match.
Distinguished Senior	Competitors who are 70 years of age and older on the first day of the match.
Military	Military personnel on current active duty orders.
Law	Full-time law enforcement officers with arrest powers.

4. Individual Classes:

Division status must be achieved before Classes are recognized.

Level I and Level II	A minimum of 5 competitors per Class (recommended)
Level III/Nationals	A minimum of 10 competitors per Class (mandatory)

APPENDIX A3 – Glossary

Throughout these rules, the following definitions apply. Where a difference in definition within the body of the rules and the definition in this Glossary exists, the definition from the Glossary will be used.

Aftermarket	Items not manufactured by, or available directly from, the Original Firearm Manufacturer. (See OFM)
Allied equipment	Holsters, magazines, speed loading devices and/or their respective pouches.
Appearing target	A target which is not visible until activated or revealed.
Array	A grouping of more than one target.
Backstop	A raised structure of sand, soil or other materials used to contain bullets.
Barrier supports	See Supporting structure.
Behind	Uprange of and within the lateral confines of the specified object. e.g. "standing behind the table" means uprange of the table and inside the lines defined by the edges of the table.
Berm	A raised structure of sand, soil or other materials used to contain bullets and/or to separate one shooting bay and/or COF from another.
Bi-Pods or similar	(Rifles only) Similar refers to monopods, tripods or other items used as such, however, they must be attached to the rifle during the COF.
Bullet	The projectile in a round intended to strike a target.
Caliber	The diameter of a bullet measured in millimeters (or thousandths of an inch).
Burst operation	More than one round can be discharged on a single pull or activation of the trigger.
Cartridge case	The main body of a round, which contains all component parts.
Closed course of fire	A course of fire is considered closed or off limits when there are no official match staff present to supervise competitor actions during stage inspection.
Compensator	A device or machining integrated into the slide or barrel to counter muzzle rise (usually by externally diverting escaping gasses).
Course of fire	(Also "course" and "COF") An expression used interchangeably with "Stage".

Cross draw	When a competitor draws with their strong hand while wearing their holster on the opposite side of the body.
Detonation	Ignition of the primer of a round, other than by action of a firing pin, where the bullet does not pass through the barrel (e.g. when a slide is being manually retracted, when a round is dropped).
Disappearing target	A target which when activated and after completing its movement is no longer available for engagement.
Discharge	See Shot.
Double action	Each pull of the trigger results in the hammer falling regardless of state prior to the pull. A trigger pull results in cocking of the hammer momentarily.
Draw	The point at which a handgun is removed or disengaged from the holster so as to allow access to any portion of the interior of the trigger guard.
Dropped gun	A condition in which a competitor loses control of their firearm. Loss of control does not require the firearm to land on the ground or other range surface or prop. It occurs anytime the firearm is no longer in control of either hand, even if it is trapped against part of the body or caught in midair.
Dry firing	The activation of the trigger and/or action of a firearm which is totally devoid of ammunition.
Dummy ammunition	Includes snap caps, empty cases, dummy rounds and any other object that resembles or duplicates a live round.
Engaging	(As in "engaging a target") A competitor is actively aiming at and firing at least one shot at a target that is within view, not through walls or other barriers/obstacles except soft cover.
Facing downrange	Not facing uprange. Any position facing side berms or backstop within 90 degrees of the median intercept of the backstop.
Facing uprange	Face and Feet pointing directly (180 degrees) away from the backstop with shoulders and hips square to the backstop. A natural "toes out" stance is acceptable and meets the standard of feet pointing directly away from the backstop as long as both feet do not point in the same direction and the rest of the position requirements are satisfied.
False start	Beginning an attempt at a COF prior to the "Start signal".
Fault line	A physical ground reference line in a course of fire which defines the limit(s) of the shooting area.

Forbidden action	A competitor action which has been expressly prohibited by the Range Master and so reflected in the Written Stage Briefing.
Freestyle	Competitors are allowed to solve the challenge presented without restriction within the rules and engage targets on an "as available for engagement basis."
Grain	A common unit of measurement used in respect of the weight of a bullet (1 grain = 0.0648 grams).
Gun case/bag	A carrying device that does not allow access to or manipulation of the trigger while fully encasing the firearm.
Handling	(As in "handling a firearm") The act of manipulating, holding, or gripping a firearm while the trigger is functionally accessible.
Holstered	The point at which a handgun is inserted or engaged into the holster so as to not allow access to any portion of the interior of the trigger guard. Holstering begins when the handgun muzzle enters the holster or trigger guard enters block.
Kneeling	A body position wherein at least one knee is in contact with the ground or stage surface.
Loaded firearm	A firearm having a live round, empty case or dummy round in the chamber or cylinder or having a live or dummy round in a magazine inserted in the firearm.
Loading	The insertion of ammunition into a firearm. Loading is completed when ammunition is inserted, and firearm is in battery (slide forward or cylinder closed) and ready to fire and the competitor's hand has been removed from the magazine or other loading device (except as may occur during establishing a normal grip on the firearm).
Location	A physical space within the boundaries of a course of fire. For the purposes of this rule, a competitor will not be considered to have changed location until both feet have moved to a new physical position.
Match Official	A person who has an official duty or function at a match, but who is not necessarily qualified as, or acting in the capacity of, a Range Official.
Movement	Taking more than one step in any direction or changing body position (e.g. from standing to kneeling, from seated to standing etc.).
Must	This means the same as "will," "shall," etc. Compliance is

	mandatory.
No-shoot(s)	Target(s) that incur penalties when hit.
Not applicable	The rule or requirement does not apply to the particular discipline, Division or match level.
NROI	National Range Officers Institute.
Obstacle	Something within a course of fire, either constructed or naturally occurring, which much be negotiated by the competitor while completing the course of fire.
Occurrence	For purposes of assessing penalties, e.g., foot faults, an occurrence is defined as shooting at an array of targets from a single location or view in a course of fire. If the competitor moves to another view or location and continues to fault, that constitutes a second occurrence.
Off limits lines	A physical reference line in a course of fire which defines an area of the range floor which is off limits to a competitor during the course of fire.
OFM	Original firearm manufacturer.
PCC	Pistol Caliber Carbine, see Appendix D for Division requirements.
Primer	The part of a round which causes a detonation or a shot to be fired.
Prone	The competitor is laying on the ground or other designated surface with the front of the chest closest to the ground.
Prototype	A firearm configuration which is not in mass production and/or is not available to the general public.
Radial tears	Tears in a cardboard target radiating outwards from the diameter of a bullet hole.
Range Official	A person who is officially serving at a match in the capacity of a Range Officer.
Range surface	The surface within a shooting bay as defined by the Course of Fire that the competitors and staff must move across. This can be the bay floor or other elements of the stage (e.g. raised platform).
REF	Range Equipment Failure.
Reloading	The replenishment or the insertion of additional ammunition into a firearm. The reload is not complete until the magazine/speed loader is fully inserted, and the firearm is in battery, (slide forward or cylinder closed and ready to fire) and the competitor's hand has been removed from the magazine or other loading device (except

	as may occur during establishing a normal grip on the firearm).
Remedial action	The term used for correcting any problem to get the firearm back in operation, such as a jam, stuck bullet, or feeding problem due to issues with the magazine, ammunition, or firearm.
Reshoot	A competitor's subsequent attempt at a course of fire, authorized in advance by a Range Officer or an Arbitration Committee.
Round	A cartridge of ammunition used in a handgun or rifle.
Securely fixed (belt)	The belt doesn't move when either the gun or a magazine is drawn from it without using both hands.
Selective action	The competitor can select either Single Action or Double Action.
Shooting box	A small shooting area (generally square) formed of four connected fault lines.
Shooting position	The physical presentation of a person's body (e.g. standing, sitting, kneeling, prone).
Shell	A cartridge of ammunition used in a shotgun.
Shot	A bullet which passes completely through the barrel of a firearm.
Should	Optional but highly recommended.
Shoulder	The shoulder is defined as the upper joint of the arm and the part of the body between the arm and the neck.
Sight picture	Aiming at a target without actually shooting at it.
Significant advantage	Any position assumed while faulting that provides:

- A greater view of a target or target array, i.e., seeing all of the array versus only one or two targets, or more of a target behind an obscuring no-shoot or wall
- A closer (more than 3 feet) shot at a target, especially if the target is partially obscured with a no-shoot or hard cover
- Less physical positioning, i.e., lean, around or over a wall or barrier
- A more stable position, such as stepping off of a moving platform or narrow beam onto the ground, provided that the object in question has been marked as a shooting area
- Having both feet outside of a shooting area and firing shots (10.2.1.2)
- Stability by bracing on a wall or barrier outside of the fault lines

Note: These are some examples and are not intended to illustrate all possible cases of significant advantage

Single action	Pulling the trigger causes the hammer to fall a single time. The hammer must be reset by other action (movement of the slide or competitor action) before it will fall again.
Snap cap	(Also "spring cap") A type of dummy round.
Squib	A bullet or solid obstruction lodged inside the barrel of a firearm.
Stance	The physical presentation of a person's limbs (e.g. hands by the side, arms crossed etc.).
Standing	The competitor's body is fully erect with both feet planted firmly on the ground or other designated position.
Start condition	The condition of the firearm prior to commencement of the course of fire, e.g., loaded, unloaded, safety applied, etc. The start condition MUST be clearly defined by the Written Stage Briefing.
Start position	The location, shooting position and stance prescribed by a COF prior to issuance of the "Start signal." The start position MUST be clearly defined by the Written Stage Briefing.
Static targets	Targets which are stationary and are not activated.
Strong hand	The hand a competitor uses to draw their handgun from their holster.
Strong side	(For long guns) Firearm is mounted to the shoulder on the strong hand side of the body and trigger must be pulled with the strong hand. A shooter must utilize the same side of the body as their strong side for the duration of the match.
Supine	The competitor is laying on the ground or other designated surface with the spinal column and shoulder blades closest to the ground. NOT recommended due to potential for sweeping.
Supporting structure	A brace, stand, rope, cable or other element used to support a barrier, line, or obstacle. These do not exist and are not part of the shooting area except as specifically stated in the Written Stage Briefing.
Sweeping	Pointing the muzzle of a firearm at any part of any person's body, while holding it in the hands, or placing it on or removing it from an object. There may be an exception for RO interference.
Target(s)	A term that can include both scoring target(s) and no-shoot(s).
Tie-down rig	A holster where the lower section is strapped or rigidly attached to a competitor's leg.
Unloading	The removal of ammunition from a firearm. This action is

	completed when the firearm is empty of all ammunition and the magazine removed or cylinder opened and shown for inspection by a Range Officer.
View	A range of sight or vision specific to an array of targets. In order to constitute a new "view" under this rule, the range of sight of an array of targets must be broken by a vision barrier of some sort, such that a different array of targets is seen in the new view.
Waist level	The normal wear level for the lower garment. Wearing a belt at waist level, which is deemed to be at the same level as the original belt loops on the lower garment means that the belt is worn at the normal wear level for the pants, trousers, skirt, kilt, shorts or jeans.
Weak hand	The hand opposite the strong hand.
Weak side	(For long guns) Opposite of Strong Side. Firearm is mounted to the shoulder on the weak hand side of the body and trigger must be pulled with the weak hand. The shooter must utilize the same side of their body as the weak side for the duration of the match.
Will	Mandatory.
WSB	Written Stage Briefing. A written briefing prepared per 3.2 read verbatim to competitors prior to their attempt on a course of fire.

Target diagrams and dimensions

Half-Size USPSA Target

Half-size IPSC Target

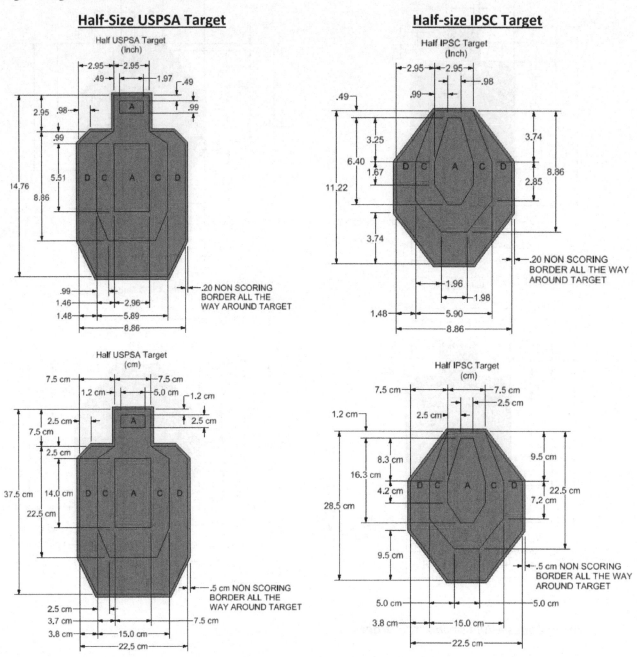

See rule 4.2.1.1 for presentation requirements for half-sized targets.

USPSA Target

IPSC Target

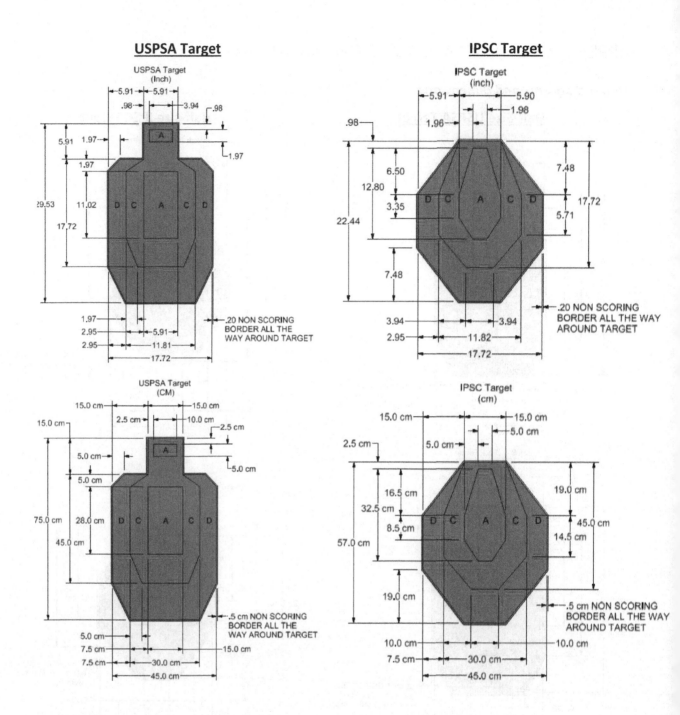

Scoring Zones – All Cardboard Targets

Scoring Zone	Major Power Factor	Minor Power Factor
A	5	5
C	4	3
D	2	1

Note that the B zone on all USPSA targets is now scored as a C hit. B zoned targets are on an indefinite phase out per BOD directive in 2018. B-zoned cardboard targets may still be used as official targets but must be scored using the A-C-D scoring listed above.

Minimum A-Zone Requirements for USPSA and IPSC Targets

<u>USPSA target:</u> At least 25% of the lower A-zone, or the entire upper A-zone, must remain visible around hard cover or overlapping no-shoots.

<u>IPSC target:</u> The minimum amount of A-zone, which must be visible in order to comply with 25% requirement is shown below.

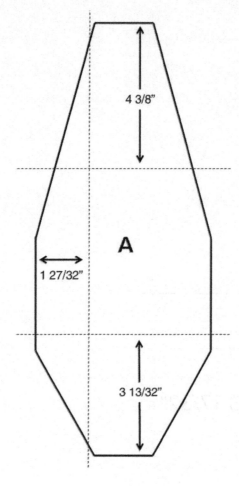

Minimum A-Zone Requirements for Half-Size USPSA and IPSC Targets

<u>*Half-Sized USPSA target:*</u> At least 50% of the lower A-zone must remain visible around hard cover or overlapping no-shoots.

<u>*Half-Sized IPSC target:*</u> The minimum amount of A-zone, which must be visible in order to comply with 50% requirement is shown below.

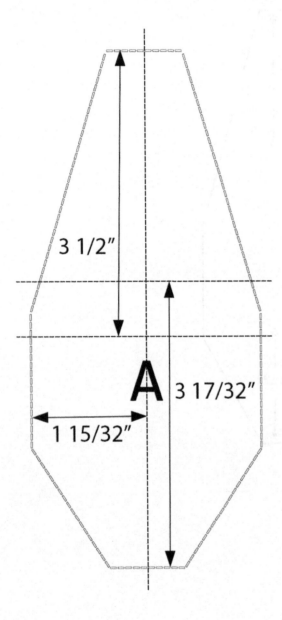

APPENDIX B2 – Popper Calibration Zones and Dimensions

The calibration zone for each target is indicated by the shaded area.
Measurement tolerance on Poppers +/- 1/4 inch.

All Poppers – Scoring value: 5 points (Minor and Major)

USPSA Mini-Popper
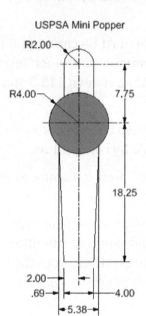

USPSA Popper
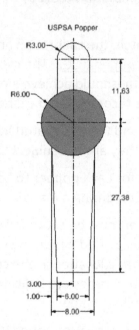

Colt Speed Steel
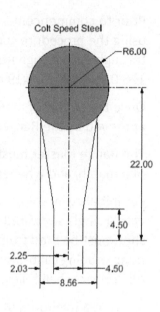

IPSC Mini-Popper
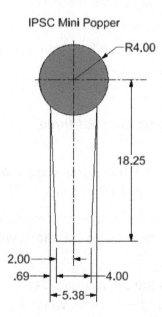

IPSC Popper
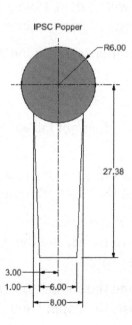

APPENDIX C1 – Calibration of Poppers

Initial Calibration

1. Any chronograph, regardless of design, is acceptable for use at all USPSA match levels, as long as the rules and guidelines stated here are followed. Always read, understand, and follow the manufacturer's recommendations.

2. The Range Master must designate a specific supply of ammunition and one or more handguns to be used as official calibration tools by officials authorized by him to serve as calibration officers.

3. Prior to commencement of a match, the calibration ammunition must be chronographed using the procedure specified in Appendix C2. The calibration ammunition, when tested through each designated handgun, should achieve a power factor between 115.0 and 125.0 to qualify. 9x19 mm is the recommended caliber.

4. Once the supply of ammunition and the designated handguns have been tested and approved by the Range Master, they are not subject to challenge by competitors.

5. The Range Master must arrange for each popper to be calibrated prior to commencement of a match, and whenever required during a match.

6. For initial calibration, each popper must be set to fall when hit within the calibration zone with a single shot fired from a designated handgun using the calibration ammunition. The shot must be fired from the shooting location in the course of fire furthest from the popper being calibrated. Calibration zones are indicated in the diagrams in Appendix B2. All Poppers shall follow the guidelines below:

   a. That a minimum of 50% of the calibration zone (100% for mini poppers) be available at some point in the COF.

   b. For handgun, the calibration will be done from a point on the COF where the is available furthest from the popper being calibrated.

   c. For shotgun or rifle, the calibration will be done with the calibration handgun from a distance of 30 feet.

Calibration Challenges

7. If, during a course of fire, a popper does not fall when hit, a competitor has three alternatives:

   a. The popper is shot again until it falls. In this case, no further action is required, and the course of fire is scored "as shot" with the subject popper scored as a hit.

   b. The popper is left standing, but the competitor does not challenge the calibration. In this case, no further action is required, and the course of fire is scored "as shot", with the subject popper scored as a miss.

   c. The popper is left standing, and the competitor challenges the calibration. (See Rule 4.3.4 for specifics.) In this case, the popper and the surrounding area on which it stands must not be touched, painted, or interfered with by any person. If a Match Official violates this rule, the competitor must reshoot the course of fire. If the competitor or any other person violates this rule, the popper will be scored as a miss and the rest of the course of fire will be scored "as shot". If the popper falls for any non-interference reason (e.g. wind action), before it can be calibrated, 4.6 will apply and a reshoot must be ordered.

8. In the absence of any interference, or problem with a target mechanism, the Range Master must first visually inspect the popper for defects or obstructions. If none are found, he must conduct a calibration test of the subject popper (when required under 7c above), from as near as possible to the point from where the competitor shot the popper for handgun, or from a distance of 30 feet for shotgun or rifle. The following will apply:

    a. If the first shot fired by the Range Master hits the popper anywhere on its frontal surface and the popper does not fall, the calibration test fails, and the competitor must be ordered to reshoot the course of fire once the popper has been recalibrated.

    b. If the first shot fired by the Range Master hits above the calibration zone, the calibration test fails, and the competitor must be ordered to reshoot the course of fire once the popper has been recalibrated.

    c. If the first shot fired by the Range Master misses the popper altogether, another shot must be fired until either 8a, 8b, or 8d occurs.

    d. If the first shot by the Range Master hits on or below the calibration zone and the popper falls, the Range Master shall require the popper to be reset to its upright position and repeat the calibration process per 8a, 8b, and 8c above. If the popper falls to the calibration shot once again, the popper is deemed to be properly calibrated, and it will be scored as a miss. It is strongly suggested that the RM request the person originally setting the popper to reset it, to determine if that action may have caused the popper to function improperly.

9. Note that authorized metal plates are not subject to calibration or challenge (see Rule 4.3.5).

APPENDIX C2 – Chronograph

Match Chronograph and Equipment Set-up

Chronograph(s):

1. The chronograph(s) must be shielded from the effects of changing sunlight. Setting the chronograph(s) in the shade of a tree, or under a cover which allows a differing amount of sunlight to touch any part of the skyscreens or skyscreen brackets is prohibited. The recommended method for outdoor locations is to use an enclosed "chrono box". In all locations, the use of either infrared sensors or incandescent lighting provides the most consistent, repeatable results. USPSA does not require a specific brand or type of chronograph. Radar sensing units are acceptable, provided they are set up and operated according to the manufacturer's directions for use and verified daily using the procedure outlined in section 17.

2. Two chronographs should be used when possible and set up in tandem so both units measure each shot fired.

3. In all cases, the skyscreens must be positioned and spaced per the manufacturer's requirements for the chronograph in use. The closest skyscreen must be placed no less than 10 feet from the shooting location (measured from muzzle of firearm to skyscreen). When radar sensing units are used, the reading at V0 must be used.

4. When possible, the chronograph(s) should be run on AC power. If using generator power, the chronograph readings must be monitored for consistency. If using battery power, the battery must be changed or recharged as necessary to insure consistent results.

5. Failing these conditions, or in the absence of a chronograph, the match must use each competitor's declared Power Factor for match scoring.

Scale(s):

6. Scales must be shielded from the wind to prevent errors in measurement while weighing competitor bullets.

7. Two scales are recommended when available, weighing each bullet tested on both scales.

8. Whenever possible, the scale(s) should be run on AC power. If using generator power, the scale readings must be monitored for consistency. If using battery power, the batteries must be changed or recharged as necessary to insure consistent results

9. A set of appropriate check weights must be used in calibrating the scale(s).

10. Failing these conditions, or if a scale is not available, each competitor's declared bullet weight must be used.

11. If a division as listed in Appendix D requires weighing of a handgun, the same procedure as above will be followed.

Bullet Puller(s):

12. Bullet pullers must be of a design which will not damage the bullet or change its weight.

13. If a bullet puller is not available or breaks and a replacement is not available, the declared bullet weight must be used for all subsequent competitors.

Calibration Ammunition:

14. A sufficient supply of match calibration ammunition must be available and used to calibrate steel targets and (when necessary) verify the match chronograph.

15. To assure consistency, the match calibration ammunition should be comprised of ammunition from the same lot. 9x19 mm is the recommended caliber.

16. The ammunition, as fired through each designated handgun, should achieve a power factor between 115.0 and 125.0.

Match Chronograph Daily Verification

Chronograph(s):

17. Prior to performing any competitor ammunition testing, the Chrono Officer will fire three rounds from the supply of the official match calibration ammunition through the calibration firearm over the chronograph(s) and record the average velocity of the three rounds for each chronograph in use.

18. Dual chronograph configurations are not subject to subsequent daily verification provided that the differential of the velocities between the two chronographs remains reasonably consistent with the differential of the average velocities recorded above.

19. For single chronograph configurations, or whenever one of the dual chronographs fails and cannot be replaced, the single functioning chronograph is subject to subsequent daily verification check. Specifically:

    a. On each of the following days, the process specified in Item 17 will be repeated using the same firearm and ammunition supply.

    b. The chronograph is deemed to be within tolerance if the daily average is within +/- 4% of the first day's average.

20. Should a daily variance exceed the allowable tolerance above, the Range Master will take whatever steps necessary to rectify the situation. If more than one chronograph is in use, and only one is out of tolerance, that chronograph can be removed from service and the remaining chronograph can be used alone for the rest of the match.

21. If the Range Master determines that variances or malfunctions make further testing unreliable or impossible, the power factors of competitors who have been successfully tested will stand. The power factors declared by all competitors who have not been tested will be accepted without challenge, subject to any applicable Division requirements.

Scale(s):

22. Daily, prior to weighing any competitor bullets, the Chrono Officer will calibrate each scale using the scale's supplied calibration weights per the manufacturer's instructions, following which the scale will be zeroed and a designated check weight(s) will be weighed

on each scale and the results recorded.

Daily, prior to weighing any competitor handgun, the Chrono Officer will calibrate each scale using the scale's supplied calibration weights per the manufacturer's instructions, following which the scale will be zeroed and a designated check weight(s) will be weighed on each scale and the results recorded.

23. For the duration of the match, a scale is considered to be in tolerance if:

    a. the scale is able to maintain a weight display stability of +/- 0.1 grain (0.2 ounces in the case of a handgun scale) over a 15 second period, and

    b. the scale is able to repeat the results of the recorded weights in Item 22 within +/- 0.1 grain, 0.2 ounces in the case of a handgun scale.

24. A scale suspected or found to be out of tolerance will be reset (calibrated and zeroed) and demonstrate satisfactory tolerance prior to being returned to service. Any competitor suspecting a scale is out of tolerance may request that the Range Master be summoned for a ruling.

25. A scale failing Item 23a must be checked for effective wind protection and stable positioning prior to reset.

26. If it is determined that a scale is unable to remain within tolerance or has failed, it must be removed from use. A replacement scale may be utilized if it can be calibrated, zeroed, and be demonstrated to be in tolerance.

27. If more than one scale is in use, and one has failed, the remaining scale can be used alone for the rest of the match.

28. If the Range Master determines that variances or malfunctions make further weight testing unreliable or impossible, the bullet or gun weights declared by all competitors whose bullets or guns have not been weighed will be accepted without challenge, subject to any applicable Division requirements.

Competitor Ammunition Collection and Storage

29. An initial sample of eight rounds of ammunition will be collected from each competitor at a time and place determined by Match Officials. Match Officials may require that a competitor's ammunition be retested at any time during the match and may collect further samples as necessary.

30. It is recommended that ammunition be collected from competitors as randomly as is possible to ensure that the collected ammunition accurately matches the ammunition the competitor is actually using in competition.

31. Collected ammunition must be clearly labeled with the competitor's identity.

32. Collected ammunition must be stored in a shaded location, out of the direct effects of the sun. When stored overnight, collected ammunition must be stored indoors at normal room temperature.

Competitor Ammunition Testing Procedure

33. Ammunition must be tested using the competitor's firearm. Prior to and/or during testing, the competitor's firearm and the component parts thereof must not be altered or modified in any way from the condition it is being used (or will be used) at the match. Violations will be subject to Section 10.6.

34. Conventions to be used for all measurements:

    a. if more than one chronograph is in use, the highest velocity recorded by any of the chronographs shall be used for each respective shot.

    b. if more than one scale is in use concurrently, the highest weight measured by the scales shall be used for each respective bullet weighed.

35. From the eight sample rounds drawn by Match Officials, one bullet is weighed to determine the actual bullet weight and three bullets are fired over the chronograph. Digits displayed on the official match bullet scales and chronograph will be used at face value, irrespective of the number of decimal places indicated on the measuring device used at the match.

36. Power factor is calculated using the bullet weight and the average velocity of the three rounds fired, according to the following formula:

    Power Factor = bullet weight (grains) x average velocity (feet per second) / 1000

    The final result will ignore all decimal places (e.g. for USPSA purposes, a result of 124.9999 is not 125).

37. If the resultant power factor fails to meet the declared power factor score, another round will be fired over the chronograph and the scores recalculated using the bullet weight and the average top three highest velocities of the number of shots fired. This will continue until either the competitor meets the minimum power factor or until all 6 rounds have been fired.

38. If the power factor is still insufficient, the competitor may elect to have:

    a. the final bullet pulled and weighed and, if heavier than the first bullet, the power factor calculation in Paragraph 36 will be recalculated using the heavier bullet weight, or

    b. the final round fired over the chronograph and the power factor recalculated using the first bullet weight, and the average velocity of the three highest velocity rounds from the seven rounds fired.

39. If the resultant power factor fails to meet the Major power factor floor of the relevant Division, the competitor's entire match scores will be recalculated as Minor, if achieved.

40. If the resultant power factor fails to meet the minimum power factor floor for the relevant Division, the competitor may continue shooting the match, but not for score or match recognition.

41. Due to the different methods used by certain chronograph brands to calculate Power

Factor, any power factor results produced by the Chrono Station chronograph are considered interim results and subject to confirmation.

a. The only official power factor results are produced and/or confirmed by using the formula specified in Item 36 or via the scoring program.

42. If a competitor's match ammunition is retested, or if any authorized replacement ammunition is used, and different power factors are recorded when tested according to these rules, the lower power factor must be applied to all courses of fire, including those already completed by the competitor.

43. The scores of a competitor who, for any reason, fails to present his firearm for testing at the designated time and location and/or who fails to provide sample rounds for testing whenever requested by a Match Official will be removed from the match results.

Chronograph Station Rules and Policies

44. The Chronograph Station is considered an official stage in the match and subject to all sections of this rule book.

45. The Chrono Officer is the CRO for the chronograph stage and issues range commands appropriate to the requirements of the Chrono Station.

46. Shooters are prohibited from handling their handgun except as specifically required to do so by the Chrono Officer.

47. Unless otherwise authorized by the Chrono Officer, once the firearm and magazine are surrendered for testing neither may be removed from the Chrono Station until the testing is complete.

48. The Chrono Officer will inspect the competitor's firearm and associated equipment and report any failure of the following to the Range Master:

a. Proper function of the firearm's primary safety mechanism(s)
b. Safe condition and operation
c. Compliance with the requirements of the declared Division

49. At the command of the Chrono Officer, the competitor may be required to fire up to six rounds into a designated target or spot on the berm/backstop prior to the competitor's ammunition sample being tested through the chronograph.

50. The Chrono Officer will perform the competitor ammunition testing procedure as specified above and enter the results on a score sheet suitable for such use.

51. Following testing, should the interim chronograph results be close to the minimum applicable Power Factor floor, it is recommended that any remaining rounds of the competitor's sample ammunition be secured and retained at the Chrono Station for potential later reference or additional testing.

52. A recommended procedure to follow at the chronograph station is to advise the squad/individual competitors via Written Stage Briefing to not to handle the firearm until instructed. The Chronograph CRO should have a station next to him where the

competitor, when called, can step up and when instructed to MAKE READY, show a cleared firearm and then place it on the table per the CRO's instructions. The competitor will also provide an empty magazine and may be asked for the longest magazine used in the match. The competitor will then step back until the chronograph process is completed. The Chronograph CRO, after the ammo has been tested, will make sure the firearm is empty and then place it on the table and call the competitor to UNLOAD AND SHOW CLEAR, followed by IF CLEAR, HAMMER DOWN, AND HOLSTER. The empty magazine will be returned at this time and the next competitor called to the line.

APPENDIX C3 – Certified Ammunition

Competitors using Certified Ammunition are exempt from the requirements of Appendix C2, Items 39 and 40 as appropriate for the declared power factor provided the delivery sample passes the Ammo Verification process and no substitutions have been made.

Source of Ammo	Ammo may be delivered to the competitor only at the match where it will be used and designated official by the US Regional Director. Ammo purchased at retail from a commercial source by competitors may also be designated as Certified Ammunition, provided the manufacturer has provided required data and samples to USPSA for inspection and testing, per the Certified Ammunition Policy, set by the USPSA Board of Directors. All other Certified Ammunition requirements, including delivery and chronograph samples, will apply.
Power Factor	Specific ammo products may be certified as meeting Minor or Major power factor for specific divisions by the US Regional Director.
Competitor Declaration	A competitor who wishes to use Certified Ammo at the certified power factor must file a declaration with the Match Director stating the Certified Ammo product will be in use for the entire match. This declaration must be filed before starting the match.
Withdrawal of Declaration	A competitor who has declared he is using only Certified Ammo may withdraw the declaration by informing the Range Master prior to use of any non-certified ammo.
Ammo Samples	At any match where competitor ammunition will be chronographed, a competitor using Certified Ammo will be required to provide eight rounds of this ammo at the time they pick up the ammo (delivery sample) and will also be subject to the provisions of Appendix C2, Item 29.
Ammo Verification	At any match where competitor ammunition will be chronographed, a competitor using Certified Ammo will have ammo samples collected during the match and chronographed according to the provisions of Appendix C2, Item 29. Should the ammo so tested fail to meet the declared power factor, it shall be compared against the average of three rounds collected from the official delivery sample. If the samples collected during the match measure more than 10 power factor points below the delivery samples, the measured power factor of the ammo collected during the match shall be used for score and the provisions of Appendix C2, Item 39 or Item 40 shall apply.
Unsportsmanlike Conduct	The use of ammo other than Certified Ammunition, while declaring use of Certified Ammunition, shall be considered unsportsmanlike conduct.

APPENDIX D1 – Open Division

		Handgun	Rifle	Shotgun	PCC
1	Firearm type restrictions	NO	NO	NO	NO
2	Action type restrictions	NO	NO	NO	NO
3	Minimum caliber/Cartridge	.354 or 9MM / 9x19 mm	5.45mm x 39mm	20 gauge	Approved/ Permitted Calibers: 9mm, .357 Sig, .40 S&W, 10mm, .45 ACP
4	Power factor min. for Major (Hit Factor scoring only)	165	320	N/A	N/A
5	Power factor min. for Minor (Hit Factor scoring only)	125	150	N/A	125, Max 1600 FPS
6	Minimum caliber for Major (Hit Factor scoring only)	.354 or 9MM / 9x19 mm	None	20 gauge	N/A
7	Minimum bullet weight for Major (Hit Factor scoring only)	112	None	N/A	N/A
8	Maximum ammo capacity	NO	NO	NO	NO
9	Maximum Magazine length	171.25 mm	NO	NO	NO
10	Barrel porting allowed	YES	YES	YES	YES
11	Compensators allowed	YES	YES	YES	YES
12	Optical sights	YES	YES	YES	YES
13	Lasers/Flashlights attached	YES	YES	YES	YES
14	Use of Bipods and similar	YES	YES	YES	YES
15	Suppressors allowed	NO	NO	NO	NO
16	Speed loading devices	YES	YES	YES	YES

Special Conditions:

1. For all firearms (as applicable), full auto/burst fire triggers, and bump stocks are allowed but may only be used in semi-auto mode. Bump stocks must be fixed to preclude bump stock type function. See 10.5.18 for penalties. Use of binary triggers (firing once on trigger pull and once on release) is prohibited.

2. For all long guns (R, SG, and PCC), Short Barreled Rifles (SBR's) are permitted provided the competitor is in full compliance with all state and federal laws and regulations concerning ownership and transport of the SBR and the PCC otherwise complies with Divisional requirements.

3. A PCC must have a stock attached and be capable of being fired from the shoulder position. Sig Brace or any variant thereof is not allowed. Handgun conversions are allowed as long as

the conversion is shot as a PCC. Flash hiders and slings on a PCC are permitted in all divisions. For PCC, no magazine couplers are allowed. End-to-end coupling is allowed. Magazines must be carried on the belt or in apparel pockets. A PCC may be included as a separate firearm type in a match. It will not be allowed as a substitute for another firearm required in a match such as a rifle or handgun.

APPENDIX D2 – Tactical Division

		Handgun	Rifle	Shotgun	PCC
1	Firearm type restrictions	Yes – Limited Pistol Rules	NO	NO	NO
2	Action type restrictions	NO	NO	NO	NO
3	Minimum caliber/Cartridge	.354 or 9MM / 9x19 mm	5.45mm x 39mm	20 gauge	Approved/ Permitted Calibers: 9mm, .357 Sig, .40 S&W, 10mm, .45 ACP
4	Power factor min. for Major (Hit Factor scoring only)	165	320	N/A	N/A
5	Power factor min. for Minor (Hit Factor scoring only)	125	150	N/A	125, Max 1600 FPS
6	Minimum caliber for Major (Hit Factor scoring only)	.40 / 10 mm / .357 SIG	None	20 gauge	N/A
7	Minimum bullet weight for Major (Hit Factor scoring only)	None	None	N/A	N/A
8	Maximum ammo capacity	NO	NO	Maximum of 9 at start signal	NO
9	Maximum Magazine length	141.25 mm 171.25 mm for Single Stack	NO	N/A	NO
10	Barrel porting allowed	NO	NO	NO	YES
11	Compensators allowed	NO	YES Max 1" x 3" See App. E2	NO	YES
12	Optical sights	NO	YES Maximum of 1	NO	YES
13a	Lasers/Flashlights attached	Laser-NO USE/ Flashlight-YES	NO	NO	YES
14	Use of Bipods and similar	NO	NO	NO	NO
15	Suppressors allowed	NO	NO	NO	NO
16	Speed loading devices	YES	YES	NO	YES

Special Conditions:

1. For all firearms (as applicable), full auto/burst fire triggers, and bump stocks are allowed but may only be used in semi-auto mode. Bump stocks must be fixed to preclude bump stock

type function. See 10.5.18 for penalties. Use of binary triggers (firing once on trigger pull and once on release) is prohibited.

2. For all long guns (R, SG, and PCC), Short Barreled Rifles (SBR's) are permitted provided the competitor is in full compliance with all state and federal laws and regulations concerning ownership and transport of the SBR and the PCC otherwise complies with Divisional requirements.

3. A PCC must have a stock attached and be capable of being fired from the shoulder position. Sig Brace or any variant thereof is not allowed. Handgun conversions are allowed as long as the conversion is shot as a PCC. Flash hiders and slings on a PCC are permitted in all divisions. For PCC, no magazine couplers are allowed. End-to-end coupling is allowed. Magazines must be carried on the belt or in apparel pockets. A PCC may be included as a separate firearm type in a match. It will not be allowed as a substitute for another firearm required in a match such as a rifle or handgun.

APPENDIX D3 – Limited Division

		Handgun	Rifle	Shotgun	PCC
1	Firearm type restrictions	Yes – Limited Pistol Rules	NO	NO	NO
2	Action type restrictions	NO	NO	NO	NO
3	Minimum caliber/Cartridge	.354 or 9MM / 9x19 mm	5.45mm x 39mm	20 gauge	Approved/ Permitted Calibers: 9mm, .357 Sig, .40 S&W, 10mm, .45 ACP
4	Power factor min. for Major (Hit Factor scoring only)	165	320	N/A	N/A
5	Power factor min. for Minor (Hit Factor scoring only)	125	150	N/A	125, Max 1600 FPS
6	Minimum caliber for Major (Hit Factor scoring only)	.40 / 10 mm / .357 SIG	None	20 gauge	N/A
7	Minimum bullet weight for Major (Hit Factor scoring only)	None	None	N/A	N/A
8	Maximum ammo capacity	NO	NO	Maximum of 9 at start signal	NO
9	Maximum Magazine length	141.25 mm 171.25 mm for Single Stack	NO	N/A	NO
10	Barrel porting allowed	NO	NO	NO	YES
11	Compensators allowed	NO	YES Max 1" x 3" See App.E2	NO	YES
12	Optical sights	NO	YES 1 Non-Magnifying	NO	YES
13	Lasers/Flashlights attached	Laser-NO USE/ Flashlight-YES	NO	NO	YES
14	Use of Bipods and similar	NO	NO	NO	NO
15	Suppressors allowed	NO	NO	NO	NO
16	Speed loading devices	YES	YES	NO	YES

Special Conditions:

1. For all firearms (as applicable), full auto/burst fire triggers, and bump stocks are allowed but

may only be used in semi-auto mode. Bump stocks must be fixed to preclude bump stock type function. See 10.5.18 for penalties. Use of binary triggers (firing once on trigger pull and once on release) is prohibited.

2. For all long guns (R, SG, and PCC), Short Barreled Rifles (SBR's) are permitted provided the competitor is in full compliance with all state and federal laws and regulations concerning ownership and transport of the SBR and the PCC otherwise complies with Divisional requirements.

3. A PCC must have a stock attached and be capable of being fired from the shoulder position. Sig Brace or any variant thereof is not allowed. Handgun conversions are allowed as long as the conversion is shot as a PCC. Flash hiders and slings on a PCC are permitted in all divisions. For PCC, no magazine couplers are allowed. End-to-end coupling is allowed. Magazines must be carried on the belt or in apparel pockets. A PCC may be included as a separate firearm type in a match. It will not be allowed as a substitute for another firearm required in a match such as a rifle or handgun.

APPENDIX D4 – Heavy Metal Tactical Division

		Handgun	Rifle	Shotgun	PCC
1	Firearm type restrictions	Yes – Limited Pistol Rules	NO	NO	NO
2	Action type restrictions	NO	NO	NO	NO
3	Minimum caliber/Cartridge	.40 / 10 mm / .357 SIG	.308 Winchester 7.62 x 51 NATO	12 gauge	Approved/ Permitted Calibers: 9mm, .357 Sig, .40 S&W, 10mm, .45 ACP
4	Power factor min. for Major (Hit Factor scoring only)	165	320	N/A	N/A
5	Power factor min. for Minor (Hit Factor scoring only)	125	150	N/A	125, Max 1600 FPS
6	Minimum caliber for Major (Hit Factor scoring only)	.40 / 10 mm / .357 SIG	.308	12 gauge	N/A
7	Minimum bullet weight for Major (Hit Factor scoring only)	None	None	N/A	N/A
8	Maximum ammo capacity	NO	NO	Maximum of 9 at start signal	NO
9	Maximum Magazine length	141.25 mm 171.25 mm for Single Stack	NO	N/A	NO
10	Barrel porting allowed	NO	NO	NO	YES
11	Compensators allowed	NO	YES Max 1" x 3" See App.E2	NO	YES
12	Optical sights	NO	YES Maximum of 1	NO	YES
13	Lasers/Flashlights attached	Laser-NO USE/ Flashlight-YES	NO	NO	YES
14	Use of Bipods and similar	NO	NO	NO	NO
15	Suppressors allowed	NO	NO	NO	NO
16	Speed loading devices	YES	YES	NO	YES

Special Conditions:

1. For all firearms (as applicable), full auto/burst fire triggers, and bump stocks are allowed but may only be used in semi-auto mode. Bump stocks must be fixed to preclude bump stock

type function. See <u>10.5.18</u> for penalties. Use of binary triggers (firing once on trigger pull and once on release) is prohibited.

2. For all long guns (R, SG, and PCC), Short Barreled Rifles (SBR's) are permitted provided the competitor is in full compliance with all state and federal laws and regulations concerning ownership and transport of the SBR and the PCC otherwise complies with Divisional requirements.

3. A PCC must have a stock attached and be capable of being fired from the shoulder position. Sig Brace or any variant thereof is not allowed. Handgun conversions are allowed as long as the conversion is shot as a PCC. Flash hiders and slings on a PCC are permitted in all divisions. For PCC, no magazine couplers are allowed. End-to-end coupling is allowed. Magazines must be carried on the belt or in apparel pockets. A PCC may be included as a separate firearm type in a match. It will not be allowed as a substitute for another firearm required in a match such as a rifle or handgun.

APPENDIX D5 – Heavy Metal Limited Division

		Handgun	Rifle	Shotgun	PCC
1	Firearm type restrictions	Yes – Limited Pistol Rules	NO	NO	NO
2	Action type restrictions	NO	NO	YES Pump Only	NO
3	Minimum caliber/Cartridge	.429 / 44 Special	.308 Winchester 7.62 x 51 NATO	12 gauge	Approved/ Permitted Calibers: 9mm, .357 Sig, .40 S&W, 10mm, .45 ACP
4	Power factor min. for Major (Hit Factor scoring only)	165	320	N/A	N/A
5	Power factor min. for Minor (Hit Factor scoring only)	125	150	N/A	125, Max 1600 FPS
6	Minimum caliber for Major (Hit Factor scoring only)	.429	.308	12 gauge	N/A
7	Minimum bullet weight for Major (Hit Factor scoring only)	None	None	N/A	N/A
8	Maximum ammo capacity	NO	NO	Maximum of 9 at start signal	NO
9	Maximum Magazine length	141.25 mm 171.25 mm for Single Stack	NO	N/A	NO
10	Barrel porting allowed	NO	NO	NO	YES
11	Compensators allowed	NO	YES Max 1" x 3" See App. E2	NO	YES
12	Optical sights	NO	YES 1 Non-Magnifying	NO	YES
13	Lasers/Flashlights attached	Laser-NO USE/ Flashlight-YES	NO	NO	YES
14	Use of Bipods and similar	NO	NO	NO	NO
15	Legally owned suppressors allowed	NO	NO	NO	NO
16	Speed loading devices	YES	YES	NO	YES

Special Conditions:

1. For all firearms (as applicable), full auto/burst fire triggers, and bump stocks are allowed but may only be used in semi-auto mode. Bump stocks must be fixed to preclude bump stock type function. See 10.5.18 for penalties. Use of binary triggers (firing once on trigger pull and once on release) is prohibited.

2. For all long guns (R, SG, and PCC), Short Barreled Rifles (SBR's) are permitted provided the competitor is in full compliance with all state and federal laws and regulations concerning ownership and transport of the SBR and the PCC otherwise complies with Divisional requirements.

3. A PCC must have a stock attached and be capable of being fired from the shoulder position. Sig Brace or any variant thereof is not allowed. Handgun conversions are allowed as long as the conversion is shot as a PCC. Flash hiders and slings on a PCC are permitted in all divisions. For PCC, no magazine couplers are allowed. End-to-end coupling is allowed. Magazines must be carried on the belt or in apparel pockets. A PCC may be included as a separate firearm type in a match. It will not be allowed as a substitute for another firearm required in a match such as a rifle or handgun.

APPENDIX D6 – Modified Division (Provisional)

		Handgun	Rifle	Shotgun	PCC
1	Firearm type restrictions	Yes – Limited Pistol Rules with slide mounted optic	NO	NO	NO
2	Action type restrictions	NO	NO	NO	NO
3	Minimum caliber/Cartridge	.354 or 9MM / 9x19 mm	5.45mm x 39mm	20 gauge	Approved/ Permitted Calibers: 9mm, .357 Sig, .40 S&W, 10mm, .45 ACP
4	Power factor min. for Major (Hit Factor scoring only)	N/A	320	N/A	N/A
5	Power factor min. for Minor (Hit Factor scoring only)	125	150	N/A	125, Max 1600 FPS
6	Minimum caliber for Major (Hit Factor scoring only)	N/A	None	20 gauge	N/A
7	Minimum bullet weight for Major (Hit Factor scoring only)	N/A	None	N/A	N/A
8	Maximum ammo capacity	NO	NO	Maximum of 13 at start signal	NO
9	Maximum Magazine length	141.25 mm 171.25 mm for Single Stack	NO	N/A	NO
10	Barrel porting allowed	NO	NO	YES	YES
11	Compensators allowed	NO	YES Max 1" x 3" See App.E2	NO	YES
12	Optical sights	YES - Required Must be attached directly to slide between rear of slide and ejection port, and may not be mounted to the frame in any way	YES Maximum of 1	YES 1 Non- Magnifying	YES
13	Lasers/Flashlights attached	Laser-NO USE/ Flashlight-YES	YES	YES	YES

14	Use of Bipods and similar	NO	YES Must stay attached throughout stage	NO	NO
15	Suppressors allowed	NO	NO	NO	NO
16	Speed loading devices	YES	YES	NO	YES

Special Conditions:

1. For all firearms (as applicable), full auto/burst fire triggers, and bump stocks are allowed but may only be used in semi-auto mode. Bump stocks must be fixed to preclude bump stock type function. See 10.5.18 for penalties. Use of binary triggers (firing once on trigger pull and once on release) is prohibited.

4. For all long guns (R, SG, and PCC), Short Barreled Rifles (SBR's) are permitted provided the competitor is in full compliance with all state and federal laws and regulations concerning ownership and transport of the SBR and the PCC otherwise complies with Divisional requirements.

5. A PCC must have a stock attached and be capable of being fired from the shoulder position. Sig Brace or any variant thereof is not allowed. Handgun conversions are allowed as long as the conversion is shot as a PCC. Flash hiders and slings on a PCC are permitted in all divisions. For PCC, no magazine couplers are allowed. End-to-end coupling is allowed. Magazines must be carried on the belt or in apparel pockets. A PCC may be included as a separate firearm type in a match. It will not be allowed as a substitute for another firearm required in a match such as a rifle or handgun.

APPENDIX E1 – Magazine Measurement

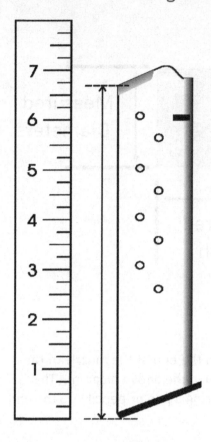

Magazine Measurement Procedure

Measurements on magazines are as follows:

5.561" (141.25 mm)
6.742" (171.25 mm)

The primary magazine measuring device shall be the EGW mag gauge. A magazine needs to conform to the length limit as well as the gauge to comply with our rules. The gauge width extends to infinity. No curved, collapsible, extendable, or similar types of magazines will be allowed. If a base pad does not conform to the configuration of the gauge, a ruler may be used to measure the overall length as pictured above.

The magazine shall be placed into the gauge without significant force or depression. It must lie so that the back of the magazine is flush against the gauge. The follower may be depressed, or slight pressure may be applied, to ensure proper fit. Some non-telescoping base pads fit loosely on the bottom of the magazine, hence the magazine may need to be "clicked in" on the mag gauge, using slight pressure.

If the magazine fit or procedure is questioned, the Range Master's call will be final.

APPENDIX E2 – Compensator Measurement

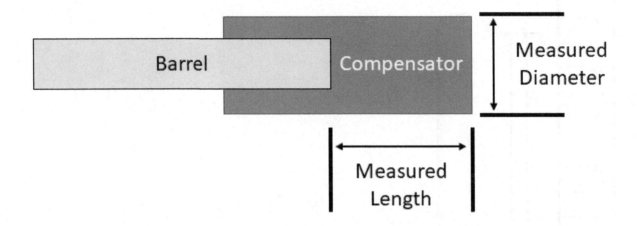

The proper way to measure the compensator length is:

The 3.00" measured length on a compensator, is measured from the end of the muzzle of the barrel to the end of the comp with the comp attached, as shown in the above diagram. This can be accomplished without removing the compensator by placing a pen or pencil into the end of the compensator until it stops at the barrel.

APPENDIX F1 – Vendor's Area

1. Vendors (i.e. individuals, corporations and other entities displaying or selling merchandise at an USPSA match) are solely responsible for the safe handling and security of their products and ensuring they are displayed in a condition that must not endanger any person. It is recommended that assembled firearms be deactivated prior to being displayed.

2. The Range Master (in consultation with the Match Director) must clearly delineate the vendor area and he may issue "Acceptable Practice Guidelines" to all vendors, who are responsible for their implementation in respect of their own merchandise.

3. Competitors may handle unloaded vendor's firearms while remaining wholly within the vendor areas, provided reasonable care is taken to ensure that the muzzle is not pointed at any person while being handled.

4. Competitors must not handle their competition firearms in the vendor's area (see Rule 10.5.1). Competitors seeking gunsmithing services for their competition firearms must first place them in a bag or case in a designated safety area before passing them to a vendor in the vendor area.

Made in the USA
Las Vegas, NV
16 February 2024

85860282R00063